# The
# Weekend Camper

# Authors' Other Books

*A Family Guide to Saltwater Fishing*
*Family Fun On and Around the Water* (WITH NORMAN STRUNG)
*The Fisherman's Almanac* (WITH NORMAN STRUNG)
*The Pennysaver Cookbook*
*The Complete Outdoor Cookbook*
*The Savor of the Sea* (WITH MATILDA MOORE)
*The Hong Kong Cookbook* (WITH ARTHUR LEM)
*The Sterling Cookbook*
*The Mike Douglas Cookbook*
*The Complete Fish Cookbook*

# THE WEEKEND CAMPER

BY

## Dan & Inez Morris

The Bobbs-Merrill Company, Inc.
Indianapolis    New York

We wish to thank the following for the help they gave us in preparing the material for this book:

A very special thanks to Richard Horan of the Morsan outdoor stores; the National Safety Council; fellow writers and good friends Norman and Sil Strung; Robert Malay of The Coleman Company Inc.; Charles Paul of the Chrysler Motors Corporation; John Ebeling of Winnebago Industries Inc.; Ed Hardy of the Primus-Sievert Company; Mrs. Doris V. Erickson of the Home Economics Division of the Cooperative Extension Association, Nassau County, New York; our nieces and nephews, Dr. and Mrs. Kenneth Kraemer and Mr. and Mrs. Harry Bloksberg; Dwight Rockwell, Jr. of Grumman Allied Industries; the United States Department of the Interior.

The Bobbs-Merrill Company, Inc.
Indianapolis · New York

*This book is dedicated
to all those who would make
every day Earth Day*

# Contents

# PART IV
## Boat and Canoe Camping

# Preface

---

## A True Story

---

This is not a funny book, but we'll begin it by telling a funny story. It's about a couple of veteran campers and we tell it only because (1) it happened needlessly, (2) it might have ended in tragedy, and (3) anything as silly as this won't happen to you if you follow our philosophy of restricting weekend camping to within easy driving distance of home.

It happened to John and Jane Doe (we call them that in order to protect them from the laughter and ribbing of the many friends they've made over the years in campgrounds throughout the United States, Canada and Mexico) while homeward-bound after weeks on the road in their pickup-truck camper. And it happened on the last day.

Three hundred miles usually was the limit of a day's driving for John and Jane on any camping trip they ever had taken. But on the end of one of the most pleasant journeys of their lives, as day dawned they were 450 miles from home, and so they decided to press on until they got there.

Then, a good breakfast under their belts, coffee pot, frying pan, dishes and knives and forks washed and safely stowed away, campsite policed for stray scraps of debris they might have overlooked, John got behind the wheel of their camper and Jane on the seat beside him.

Nine hours later and still about 75 miles from home, John had had it. He pulled to the side of the road, turned to Jane and said: "You drive, I'm going to climb into the sack and take a nap." He got out of the cab, walked to the camper's rear door, climbed in, took off his shoes and stripped down to his BVDs, stretched out on a bunk, pulled a cover over him and within minutes was dead to the world.

Jane, totally out of sight and without means of communication with John in the back compartment, tooled merrily down the highway thinking nice thoughts of spending that night in the coziness of their long-unseen home—until suddenly she came to a fork in the road and did not know which to take, left or right.

She did what any driver would do under such circumstances—came to a stop to ponder the problem. But so abruptly that John was tossed from his bunk and onto the floor of the camper. His mind befogged by sleep, he jumped to his feet, plowed through the rear door and, sockless, shoeless, shirtless and clad only in his shorts, leaped down into the road to find out what was going on.

And just then, having made up her mind, Jane took off again, oblivious to what was going on behind her. John shouted, screamed, cried, raced after her.

"Jane! Jane! Stop! Stop!"

But Jane did not hear nor did she stop, and as the camper faded into the distance, passing motorists slowed and stared at John, wondered what kind of nut was this, and sped off again.

To one or two he raised his thumb, wondering at the coldness, the cruelty, the animosity of drivers who would not give a man a lift. And then, for the first time, he came fully awake and aware of what little he wore. No socks, no shoes, no undershirt, only shorts. Quickly then he hopped behind some bushes hoping that a police car would come along that he could flag down.

But none came, the sun was fading and John was growing colder. So, stifling his embarrassment, he once more stepped to the side of the road and bravely signaled for a lift. Again car after car slowed, stared and sped off again until finally a truck came along and stopped.

"Buddy," the driver said, "you look like you're in trouble. Hop in."

John did, told his story, and the driver, a sympathetic man, stripped off his jacket and said: "Here, buddy, you wear this and we'll go find your wife."

He stepped on the gas, tooled down the road to catch the long-gone camper and so an hour or more went by and they were at a cutoff 15 miles from John's home.

"She must be there by now," he said. "I'll get out here."

"Not on your life," the truck driver said. "I'll take you."

And he did. But when they got there, Jane was not.

John thanked him, invited him in for a drink, heard him decline, took his name and address so he could properly say thank you by mail and perhaps with a gift, climbed down from the cab, waved goodbye, walked up the walk to the front door, to the rear door and then to every window that he could reach. They all, of course, were locked.

But, luckily, the garage doors were not. So John opened them wide, unfolded a garden chair and sat down inside, safe from prying passing eyes, to wait for Jane.

He sat and he sat and slowly became aware that the lawn was parched, more brown than green, and badly in need of watering—this, John, an amateur gardener who took great pride in his grass and his flowers, could not stand.

John rationalized. They live in a sparsely settled area. Houses are few and far between. He'd worked in the yard before in bathing trunks. If any neighbors should see him maybe they'd think he was wearing bathing trunks once again.

Thus mentally fortified, he hooked up the garden hose, turned on the valve and proceeded to give the lawn a long-overdue watering.

And that was what he was doing when Jane, who thought him still asleep in the camper, came home several wrong turns later. She turned into the driveway, saw him, let out a shriek, rammed her foot down on the gas pedal instead of the brake, drove into the garage, through the rear wall and out again. Luckily she was unhurt.

And so our camping story ends.

*Moral:* Never drive more than 300 miles a day on a camping trip; 50 to 200 miles if on an overnight or weekend camping trip.

*Moral:* Study a road map and become familiar with every turn before starting each day's drive.

*Moral:* Never ride in the back of a camper or trailer; sit up front with the driver.

*Moral:* Have rear-vision mirrors on both sides of recreational vehicles. And use them constantly. Know what's going on behind you as well as in front of you.

# The Illustrations
# Can Be Useful

Developed and adopted by the National Park Service in cooperation with the United Nations, the picture symbols which appear on the jacket and throughout this book were put there not just because they are very decorative, but, more important, because they are useful to all campers. Become familiar with these symbols and you will find it easier to locate the facilities you want throughout the entire national park system and hopefully ultimately throughout the world. We hope too that all fifty American states post them in their parks and forests.

These symbols will all have the same color scheme: white on brown, grey-blue or green. A red slash-mark across the symbol indicates that the activity is prohibited.

# The
# Weekend Camper

# PART I

# The Who, Why, What, When and Where of Weekend Camping

# Chapter 1

# Everyone Can Be
# a Weekend Camper

As our civilized lives grow more complex, our yearning to return to what was once a simpler, closer-to-nature way of life increases. Camping is the only way most of us have to satisfy that yearning.

Camping, fortunately, is for everyone with a will to break completely away from the tensions of the everyday routine and, instead of living in their houses, live out-of-doors—camping with the whole family no matter what the number of kids, no matter what their ages, camping alone or with friends.

This book, you might say, is a primer on the subject. Both in time and in distance a camping trip can be as long or as short as you want it. But we don't recommend the long haul, either in time or in distance, for the beginning camper. This book will deal with only one-night camping, or at the most, two-night, because that is how to begin.

Weekend camping, overnight camping, quickie camping, call it what you will. This book will tell you how to camp simply, pleasantly, inexpensively, making do as much as possible with what you've got, spending as little as possible on camping equipment.

If you're the head of a young family with a gleam in your eye to do with your family what more and more Americans are doing every year—getting back to nature while there still is nature to get back to—there's no better way to ease your brood into active participation than by overnight or weekend camping. This is especially true if your funds are limited.

If you're one of the millions of Americans who own a recvee (recreational vehicle, meaning a trailer that you pull behind your car, a camping van, or a truck with living quarters mounted on the back and sometimes extending over the cab) and for whom the two- to four-week annual camping vacation just whets your appetite and makes you long for more, the ever-lengthening American weekend should give you what you want. But maybe you'll need to take a somewhat different approach to short weekend trips, and maybe this book will give you some ideas about the joys of camping close to home without all the fuss of preparing for a lengthy cross-country endeavor.

*Speaking of cross-country endeavor, in the next chapter we'll tell you about a type of camping that's made to order for the jet-set weekend camper. The airlines dreamed it up and it's called "Fly and Camp."*

Maybe you're a couple who have put in years of hard work looking forward to the days when you could get out into the open, feel the meaning of life close about you, see some of the grandeur of America's great out-of-doors—but inflation has sadly dwindled your retirement funds, so those long trips in a new recvee are out of the question. Take heart. Weekend camping can be the answer for you, just as for the young family beginning its life with limited funds.

And we think that you will both find more of the real meaning of camping in the sort of living outside that can be done on a shoestring than you might find in struggling through some of the recvee problems that are developing as more ordinances are written affecting them.

Just about anyone, except the hopelessly helpless or infirm, can be a one-night or two-night camper, because there is some kind of camping for everyone. You should be in reasonably good health, of course, but beyond that it makes little difference. If you're able to get in and out of a car, with or without assistance, you're able to camp out overnight. Even folks with canes, folks on crutches, and folks in wheelchairs can.

Age makes no difference. We know of camps in the United States that are laid out with older folks in mind, and we know doddery old graybeards who camp there. We also know parents who take their five-month-old daughter camping.

The fact is that disabilities don't count; it's a person's abilities and determination that matter, and there's a pilot company (Abilities Inc. is its name) that employs only the physically handicapped to prove it. And there are campgrounds that are built expressly to help the handicapped get around. One such is in California's Inyo National Forest, and you can thank the Mammoth Lakes Lions Club for being its prime spark plug.

Yes, overnight or weekend camping is for everyone. The needs are minimal, and in certain cases (which we will tell you about later) perhaps even nil. The price you pay is strictly up to you. If you like your luxuries to come plush, there is that kind of camping too. You can camp in all the comfort you want, what with all the vehicles and equipment available to anyone who wants to pay the price.

But this we can tell you from personal experience and the experience of friends: If your eyelids are beginning to twitch and your nerves are hair triggers from mental fatigue, a little bit of roughing it is apt to be the best medicine for what ails you—just enough to occupy your mind completely, so you don't have time to budget and brood and you're so *physically* tired come bedtime that you fall immediately into a deep sleep.

Inez once developed a twitch in her eyelid from nervous fatigue. She went around with her eyes cast down because she never knew when or at whom she'd inadvertently wink, and a lady can get into all sorts of difficulty that way. The kids were young at the time and Inez was a Girl Scout leader. When a camping weekend came up she had almost decided she was too tired to go. But she went. The temperature suddenly dropped to 35 and it rained the whole weekend. Gathering wood, drying out, building fires and shelters, just keeping fed and warm kept everybody busy. No time to think about family illnesses or school experiments that were turning our kids into guinea pigs. She came home without the twitch.

Dan had a stroke about 18 years ago which we have sometimes referred to as his "stroke of good luck." Impossible for a stroke to be lucky, you say? Not at all, because it forced him to revive his youthful interest in physical activity that has undoubtedly helped keep him alive and well for those subsequent 18 years.

"Walk," the doctor told him, "and eat fish. Eat it four times a week instead of red meat all the time!"

So instead of taking the easy way of getting anywhere he had to go Dan forced himself to walk, and gradually the partial paralysis caused by the stroke went away. He followed the doctor's orders and ate fish instead of red meat part of the time, and brought much of it home from the ocean after an exhilarating and completely relaxing contest of fishing in the surf.

He bought a small outboard motorboat and forced himself to master the monstrous wakes of the seagoing pleasure boats that ply our Long Island inland waters, to moor the boat in spite of tricky winds and tides. Not only did he learn to moor it at a slip but also off secluded islands, meeting the challenge of the ever-changing tide. Then he took the rest of the family boat picnicking, and then just an easy overnight step further, boat camping.

You'd never know now that he'd had a stroke.

All of which is very apropos to the camping scene today. Before buying equipment, before planning trips, ask yourself: "What do I want to get from camping?"

Camping, particularly overnight or weekend family camping, can be the most economical form of outdoor recreation. Camping equipment is nice and convenient to have, but you can make do with the pots and pans that you use every day. And, yes, the bedding that you use every night.

Instead of lamenting that you can't afford all of the bright and shiny equipment just purchased by the Jones family, develop your ingenuity and take pride in it; it can add to the general feeling of well-being and fun.

*If camping equipment becomes a status symbol rather than a means to an end (and from the billions being spent on it, it looks as if that could happen unless we keep our sense of perspective), then camping will defeat its own purpose. Its true meaning, its human value that over the centuries has engendered and encouraged friendly helpfulness among* campers (*rather than materialism and rivalry*) *will be lost.*

So if you choose to travel by automotive vehicle, as most of you will, the added expense (if you use your family jalopy) need only be for the added gas and oil that you will burn and (possibly) the expense of a small tent. Yet even in transportation there need be no great added expenditure, because you should try to limit an overnight or weekend camping trip to *at the most* a 200-mile drive from home, and 100 miles is preferable.

Nor is there anything to prevent you from limiting it to 10 to 20 miles and getting there either by foot or by bicycle.

Camping is not limited to any one means of transportation. You can go camping by family sedan, station wagon, motorcycle, bicycle or boat (you'll find a whole chapter on boat camping in this book); you can go camping by subway, streetcar or bus to the end of the line; you can go camping by hitchhiking, walking, backpacking, horsebacking, canoeing, cross-country skiing, snowshoeing, flying. You can even camp out in your own backyard, which in fact is the best possible place for you to begin.

Or you can go camping in whatever kind of recreational vehicle that you may own, pickup-truck camper, tent trailer, camp wagon, camp van, motor home or houseboat—the last two can be as luxurious as you want them. Pay the price and the manufacturers will outfit them with everything but hot and cold running bourbon.

# Chapter 2

# When and Where to Go

The most difficult part of camping today isn't learning to pitch a tent, roll up a sleeping bag or start a fire. *It's finding a destination where both the camp and the highways leading to and from it aren't jam-packed full of other campers.*

However, it *is* possible to do, and in this chapter (and in the chapter on boat camping) we are going to tell you how.

## When to Go

*The best possible days to go on a one- or two-night camping trip are Tuesday, Wednesday and Thursday. Monday is good too if it isn't part of an extended weekend, because many people can't get away from work and because it's traditional to go on Friday, Saturday and Sunday. So those midweek days are the days when the highways and camps are not crowded.*

*During what we consider the best camping months of the year in many states (May, June, September and October), just before and just after busy, hot and crowded July and August, facilities are often almost empty in midweek (and they're not all crowded on weekends). Yet the weather is often at its glorious best then. There are areas of course in the southern part of our country where midwinter weather permits comfortable snow-free camping.*

We realize that for many the "weekend" must mean Saturday and Sunday, and sometimes Friday or Monday thrown in for a three-day holiday.

If you can break out of that trap and get away sometimes for one or two nights in the middle of the week, your chances of getting space in the campground of your first choice will probably go up several hundred percent. Maybe you're self-employed and all you need do is use your imagination to figure out how to shift your work around a bit. Maybe you can trade one of those Fridays or Mondays for a Tuesday or Wednesday. Maybe you can take a midweek afternoon off sometimes (pick up the children at school if it's in the spring or fall), drive to a campground not more than an hour away from home and still have time to set up camp and go for a short hike or a swim before cooking that wonderful outdoor dinner. Perhaps, if the camp is deserted, you can sleep under the stars without even pitching a tent. Then up at dawn (you'll probably enjoy its beauty so much you'll wish you could get up at dawn in the out-of-doors every morning), eat a cold breakfast with hot coffee prepared in a vacuum jar the night before and drive home before the highway is crowded with workday traffic.

So you see, although the title of this book refers to "weekend camping," when we use that term throughout this book, what we mean is any two or three days and one or two nights you may be able to break away and go camping.

If midweek just isn't possible for you, read on and you may find your answer to uncrowded camping in the suggestions on "Where to Go."

## Where to Go

FIRST PICK THE AREA

Before trying to decide on a specific campground, you should pick the general area where you think you'd enjoy going. If you have difficulty agreeing on this, remember that since you're only talking about overnight or a weekend you should be able to go often, so you can take turns (maybe even flip a coin) and everybody will be eventually satisfied.

If you are to get the greatest pleasure and relaxation from

overnight or weekend camping, there are four points you should keep in mind when choosing the area.

**The first point:** Limit to a short drive the distance from home to destination. Camping can be just as worthwhile 5 miles or 50 miles from home as it can be 500 or 5,000 miles. Distance is not the criterion. Camping is *what* you make it, more so than *where* you make it. Camping is a state of mind just as much as it is a physical experience. We know. We've camped a couple of miles from home on an isolated Long Island sandspit; we've camped high in the mountains of New Mexico and California, which are quite a continental hop, skip and jump from our house, and we love both.

So we recommend that you limit the distance of a one-night camping trip to from one block (you just might be lucky enough to live that close to a beach or park where you are allowed to camp for one night) to, at the very most, 100 miles if traveling by automotive vehicle, 10 miles if walking, 20 miles on a bicycle (experienced cyclists can easily go as far as 50 but for a first-time camping trip it's best to limit the distance), 20 miles in a small boat (meaning no more than an 18-foot outboard).

All these figures are approximate, of course, but they will give you an idea of what your mileage limitations should be for the first time out if you expect to get the most out of an overnight camping trip and return home free of tensions, completely relaxed and filled with memories to hold you for the work week that lies ahead.

Get an early start, perhaps eating a picnic breakfast along the way after you've driven for a while, and arrive at your destination in time to set up your camp before having lunch.

That gives you the entire afternoon to swim, fish, go on nature walks, explore, whatever it is that you came to the area to do. And you have the whole evening for cooking din-

ner out-of-doors, sitting around a campfire, leaning back to
look at the stars, getting acquainted with camping neighbors if any, doing whatever you want to do. Up as close to
dawn as your life-style will permit, having breakfast (and
oh, what a treat that first outdoor morning meal will be!),
cleaning up and then off for several hours more of seeing
and doing; back to camp for lunch, breaking camp, stowing
your gear, cleaning up, and then a leisurely ride home with
perhaps a stop or two at an antique barn or outdoor flea market to pick up a knickknack or a rocker or a look-what-I-
found treasure—or a pony ride for the kids.

The closer to home you've camped, the longer the time you
can spend in and around camp and the more leisurely can be
your return trip.

When you've got your feet wet, and discovered that there's
really nothing difficult about this camping thing after all,
and you are ready for a two-nighter, then you can go much
farther away from home and still have one full day to do
your thing at camp.

If you're driving, how much farther you go will depend on
how much you like to drive, what your children's driving time
limit is (young babies are much more patient on a long drive
as a rule than are two-year-olds), but you'll generally come
home more relaxed and happy if you can hold it down to
200 miles; the less, the better.

We once drove about 200 miles from our Long Island
home to the Pennsylvania Dutch country. We drove to an
area where several campgrounds with tentsites were indicated in our AAA and Rand McNally guidebooks (since it
was Tuesday and September, we didn't bother making a
reservation). We found the Pennsylvania Dutch Campsite
(our first try) just off U.S. 22 (which is *not* a throughway)
45 miles east of Harrisburg, a pleasant, wooded commercial
campground, with campsites at $2.50 a night. It was a
modern campground with flush (as well as some outhouse-
type) toilets and clean showers. It was only about one-quarter full and we had our choice of outer, isolated sites, so we
didn't bother with a tent but set up camp cots in the open.

Since we'd stopped for a rest and a picnic lunch along the
way, we set out right away to explore the nearby village of

Shartlesville on foot. Among other things we found an entertaining little museum that occupied us for an hour. We were so enticed by a Pennsylvania Dutch restaurant menu that we decided to eat there that night since the perishables we'd packed in our camp cooler were frozen and would keep easily for the next day's dinner.

We returned to camp after dinner, chatted awhile with the friendly proprietress and struck up an acquaintance with two of the other guests who showed us the interior of their large tent trailer. We walked around camp, noticing with surprise that many of the trailers and camper living quarters were unoccupied. The next morning the proprietress explained that many people from nearby cities rented space for the entire season. They left their trailers or camperbacks there and drove their cars or pickup trucks home where they stayed during the work week, returning for weekends for as long as the weather was nice.

We slept under big, bright stars that night, looking up at them through the oak trees under which we were camped. We arose early the next morning (there's just nothing to compare to the feeling of waking up in the woods at sunrise—the feel of the cool fresh air, the sounds of life beginning to stir, the aroma of the first pot of coffee beginning to brew a few campsites away). We cooked breakfast, brewing as usual an extra supply of coffee for our vacuum jar, showered, dressed, cleaned the camp and then set out to explore the charming countryside.

Some people in Shartlesville had told us to take *old* highway 22, which we did and were enchanted by the picturesque rolling hills covered with wild flowers and clean, neat farms. Here and there was a stone church on a hilltop standing guard over a pretty graveyard, and we couldn't help thinking how lucky the former citizens were to have such a pleasant last resting place.

One more point we'd like to make about keeping your destination within easy driving distance is this: Since you don't have to keep a tight schedule, plotting the course can become part of the family fun. Get an extra map (maybe mount it on an old folding game board) so the back-seat occupants can keep track of where you're going (maybe make some suggestions) enroute. The second map will save the driver from any disturbing fears that his copy will blow away, get rumpled up or lost.

**The second point:** Pick an area you can get to without driving on turnpikes or throughways. Whatever your choice of destination may be, make the ride that will get you there and home again part of your weekend camping experience. Drive at as leisurely a pace as you can. Slow down to see the sights. Stop at a farm stand or a farmers' market to make some purchases. Perhaps stop to have a picnic lunch by the side of the road or in an interesting town park.

We've been absolutely amazed at how empty of traffic secondary roads frequently are when the throughways are filled with bumper-to-bumper traffic. It's only on the secondary roads that you go through the little hamlets and actually see the beauties and the interesting things America has to offer. Stop in a store or a park and strike up a conversation with someone who lives in a town. They'll be happy to answer questions about the area and direct you to places of interest that may not be shown in your literature (famous old houses, little museums, other places of historical interest, small fairs, places you can buy locally made cheeses—we bought delicious cheese once in an antique shop). In other words, you'll find America out there at the side of the secondary roads! Speed by on the throughways and you'll never know it exists.

And if you need any further incentive, you'll seldom pay a toll charge once you get off the throughways and turnpikes.

When choosing your itinerary, the sun deserves a little consideration. If it's going to be staring you straight in the eye as soon as you start out at daybreak, maybe you'll want to start an hour before dawn. Then when the sun jabs you in the eyes, stop for breakfast (instead of eating before you leave) where you can look around or the kids can play for just as long as it takes for that round globe of fire to shrink down to size and rise a comfortable distance above the horizon.

Going home the next day, if you're heading due west into the blinding beams of the setting sun, pull off the highway where the children can run or where you can walk around and see the sights. Maybe eat your evening meal in a park (or splurge a little and go to a restaurant if you're in good eating country). Then when the sun is down and the light is right for driving, finish your journey home, which if you didn't go too far in the first place shouldn't be far away.

**The third point:** Stay away from highly publicized spots such as Yosemite and Yellowstone unless you can go there in the off season in the middle of the week. Once you start opening your eyes to the possibilities and doing a little research, your problem won't be so much finding a destination as it will be choosing between the many that are within a 200-mile radius of most American homes.

How exciting they are will depend a lot on your attitude. If your idea of fun is to be able to boast to your next-door neighbor that you too have been to the Yellowstone National Park, the Great Smoky Mountains National Park, Grand Teton and Yosemite, you'll become one of that mass of campers caught in the jam of recreational vehicles where there's obviously little room for pleasure and relaxation.

Those well-known, much talked-about and photographed places are without a doubt very exciting and very interesting. But there are many other national parks, forests and monuments, state parks and forests, city, county and civic areas—many of them with facilities for camping and many of them just as exciting and interesting as the highly publicized places. The same goes for many privately owned campgrounds, particularly those located near points of interest so that you can camp at the campground but pursue your pleasure nearby.

An effort is being made by personnel of the National Park System to limit further building of campsites in existing parks in order to preserve the natural beauty of the landscape. Instead of building more campsites, they hope that the slack will be taken up by more nearby private campgrounds—which seems to be happening. New state, town and county campgrounds also are springing up but whether fast enough to give all of us a place to pitch our tents or park our recvees remains to be seen. At the time of this writing, Humble Oil and Refining Company has opened a num-

ber of camping parks at their gas stations, and it's a pretty
safe bet that other oil companies will get into the business
too.

Of course many of these commercial facilities will be at
the edge of the busy, well-traveled highways and not what
most tent campers would want. But if they accommodate the
recvees going somewhere else in a hurry, then the more de-
sirable camping spots for more leisurely campers will be
relieved of some of their busy-season pressure.

Yet it seems there are campsites in little-known national
parks going begging. According to the Department of the
Interior, the newest challenge to vacationing Americans is
finding those parks and recreation areas which are not near-
ing their capacity of visitors.

For example, to quote from a 1971 department news re-
lease:

Just 80 miles north of Great Smoky Mountains National Park
lies Cumberland Gap National Historical Park at the meeting
place of three states: Kentucky, Tennessee and Virginia. It offers
historic traces of the Wilderness Road, hand-hewn by Daniel
Boone's men in 1775; the remains of Fort McCook, a Civil War
earthwork fortification; and Hensley Settlement, an abandoned
mountaintop town now undergoing restoration. Cumberland Gap's
campground on U.S. 58 offers 165 campsites and is seldom
crowded. Hikers will glory in the variety of available trails.

And the department also has this to say:

Striking eastward from Lake Mead National Recreation Area,
one soon comes upon Grand Canyon National Monument at the
edge of the Recreation Area. This wild, remote region has few
roads, difficult access and few visitors. Further to the east lies
the world-famous Grand Canyon National Park with large numbers of visitors roaming the South Rim area while relatively few
are found on the equally spectacular North Rim. [Inez has been
to the North Rim and agrees with that evaluation.]

The opportunity to experience the splendors of nature in the
National Park System is not restricted to areas near the more
famous landmarks of the nation. In southeastern Utah, two of the
most spectacular—and least visited—national parks await the
tourist who wants to escape the crowds.

Bryce Canyon [Inez, who was at Bryce 25 years ago, says it's almost as awe-inspiring as Grand Canyon and is amazed that it's not crowded with visitors] and Canyonlands National Parks are wonderlands of natural erosion. The precipitous cliffs and canyons were created by the waters of the rivers and streams still coursing through the canyon bottoms. The spires, arches and exotic rock formations were developed through the ages by wind erosion.

There are more sites listed in other areas of the United States showing that if the crowds spread out a little bit, there still may be, for a while at least, enough nature available to let us all partake of its splendor. We won't list any more here, since by the time you read this book, those particular parks might no longer be underused because of the publicity the Department of the Interior is giving them. But there are others, some that have not as yet been made available to the public. A grant of a quarter of a million dollars, for instance, has recently been approved for the Mescalero Apache Tribe of New Mexico to use in developing recreation and campground facilities on its reservation.

And the Department of the Interior has long-range plans for establishing recreational parks, including camping facilities near selected urban population centers.

Ferreting out for yourself the wonderlands of the less-used national and state parks, forests, monuments and campgrounds in your own area can be an exciting adventure that can give you something worthwhile to share with friends. There is a list of pamphlets and addresses that may be helpful in your search starting on page 21.

The fourth point: When choosing your destination area keep the interests of everyone in mind so each can do his thing. Well, that may be a bit too much to hope for, especially if you happen to be a family with six or seven children. But as we pointed out before in this chapter, we're not talking about a once-a-year vacation camping trip; we're talking about overnight or weekend camping, and there's no reason for not going often enough so that everyone can have a turn choosing what's to be done. Maybe if you do enough research, you *can* come up with some places where seven children and their parents can each do his own particular thing!

You might decide to go to the seashore with its treasure chest of activities: swimming, surfboarding and surf fishing,

building castles in the sand, ball playing, seashell gathering, beachcombing, making friends, making handcrafted items from the results of your beachcombing, photography, drawing pictures in the sand—and just plain lying in the sun or under an umbrella. Whew!

Or you might want to camp near a bird sanctuary in a forest with all sorts of flora and fauna and nature trails or near a formal garden with its designed pathways and terraced lawns, or on the desert when it's abloom with spring flowers.

Maybe you're a retired couple who enjoy visiting organizations for retirees in other communities. Proposed regulations provide for free "Golden Age Passports" which will admit persons 62 and older to many Federal recreation fee areas and will give them a 50 percent discount on some daily campground fees.

Or maybe you're crazy for state and county fairs or rodeos. Your destination could be such an area, and since many of these festivals take place in the fall, you may be able to camp right in the midst of colorful, changing leaves.

Or a great many people are visiting the scenes of former mining activity (for both gold and gems) and combining a search for treasure with a camping trip. Some dig for dinosaur bones.

Maybe you like to read the inscriptions on gravestones in historic graveyards. Once in western Pennsylvania—we believe it was on Route 30—we stopped to prepare sandwiches at a lovely hilly rest stop in a stand of maples. We ate sandwiches made from pumpernickel bread, lettuce and the cheese we mentioned earlier having bought at an antique shop along the way, drank ice water from our jug and shared a small box of raisins. Very good and very pleasant. Inez walked around after eating, trying to identify the wildflowers, and came upon one lone headstone with this inscription:

WILLIAM GESSNA
Co. K. 55th. Reg. Pa. Vols.
Died Aug. 14, 1895
In his 67th year

Stirs the imagination, doesn't it?

If cooking and eating is your family's bag, you may enjoy camping with friends with similar taste near a farmer's market. Make one or two trips to the market, not only buying but feasting your eyes and your olfactory senses on those top-quality, fresh-picked fruits and vegetables and cheeses and pies and jams and jellies—mmmm. If you live far-removed from fishing streams and never get enough really good fresh fish to eat, you could go camping near a fishing village and feast to your hearts' content on chowder and charcoal-broiled fish.

Speaking of fish reminds us that there are all kinds of things a wife can do while her husband fishes or vice versa. Inez doesn't care too much for the sport (she's happy to cook the fish, however, after Dan cleans them), but Dan is an avid fisherman. She enjoys being on or near the water with him and so goes prepared with the sort of things any family should have along for stretching the "doing your own thing" activities: sketch pads (when the children were little we included felt pens and crayons), cameras (one filled with color film and a Polaroid with black and white film), pocket-size bird and flower identification booklets. When our son went along the identification booklets sometimes included one for rocks—and our daughter went through a period of carrying a notebook for letter and poetry writing, and books to read. The collection of books at one period included comic books. (Why fight against comic books? Our son learned to read from them when he found the school readers too boring.)

Don't overlook hiking and bicycle riding and just plain little short walks when choosing areas. More and more trails for these activities are being made available for public use.

When writing to your state and county officials for literature, ask about trails and nature walks in your particular area. Here's a list of 29 recreation trails belonging to the National Trails System (administered by individual agencies as indicated), just to give you an idea of what's all around you that you may not have known about:

*Legend:* B—bicycle; F—foot; H—horse; M—motorized, general; SM—snowmobile; WC—wheelchair.

Alaska: PINNELL MOUNTAIN TRAIL (24 miles), F, Bureau of Land Management, USDI.

Washington: LAKE WASHINGTON BICYCLE PATH (2.5 miles), B–F, City of Seattle Department of Parks and Recreation.

Washington: LAKE WASHINGTON SHIP CANAL WATERSIDE TRAIL (1,200 feet), F, U.S. Army Corps of Engineers.

Washington: FRED CLEATOR INTERPRETIVE TRAIL (1.3 miles), F, Washington State Parks and Recreation Commission.

Oregon: TILLAMOOK HEAD TRAIL (6 miles), F, Oregon State Highway Division, State Parks and Recreation Section.

California: KING RANGE TRAIL (10 miles in 2 segments), F–H, M, Bureau of Land Management, USDI.

California: SOUTH YUBA TRAIL (6 miles), F–H, Bureau of Land Management, USDI.

California: EAST BAY SKYLINE TRAIL (14 miles), F–H, East Bay Regional Park District.

California: GABRIELINO TRAIL (28 miles), F–H, Forest Service, USDA.

Arizona: SOUTH MOUNTAIN PARK TRAIL (14 miles), B–F–H, Phoenix Parks and Recreation Department.

Colorado: HIGHLINE CANAL TRAIL (18 miles), B–F–H, South Suburban Metropolitan Recreation and Park District, Denver.

New Mexico: ORGAN MOUNTAIN TRAIL (8.7 miles), F–H, Bureau of Land Management, USDI.

South Dakota: BEAR BUTTE TRAIL (3.5 miles), F, South Dakota Department of Game, Fish and Parks, Division of Parks and Recreation.

South Dakota: SUNDAY GULCH TRAIL (4 miles), F, South Dakota Department of Game, Fish and Parks, Division of Parks and Recreation.

South Dakota: TRAIL OF SPIRITS (0.5 mile), F, South Dakota Department of Game, Fish and Parks, Division of Parks and Recreation.

Nebraska: FONTENELLE FOREST TRAIL (3.9 miles), F, Fontenelle Forest Association.

Texas: GREER ISLAND NATURE TRAIL (3 miles), F, City of Fort Worth Park and Recreation Department.

Arkansas: SUGAR LOAF MOUNTAIN NATURE TRAIL (1 mile), F, U.S. Army Corps of Engineers.

Wisconsin: ELROY-SPARTA TRAIL (30 miles), B–F–SM, Wisconsin Department of Natural Resources, Bureau of Parks and Recreation.

Wisconsin: ICE AGE GLACIAL TRAIL (25 miles), F–SM, Wisconsin Department of Natural Resources, Bureau of Parks and Recreation.

Illinois: ILLINOIS PRAIRIE PATH (12.5 miles), B–F–H, The Illinois Prairie Path, Inc.

Kentucky: LONG CREEK TRAIL (0.25 mile), F–WC, Tennessee Valley Authority.

Tennessee: LAUREL-SNOW TRAIL (8 miles), F, Bowaters Southern Paper Corporation.

Georgia: STONE MOUNTAIN TRAIL (6.51 miles), F, Stone Mountain Memorial Park Association.

District of Columbia: FORT CIRCLE PARKS TRAIL (7.9 miles in 2 segments), B–F, National Park Service, USDI.

Pennsylvania: FAIRMOUNT PARK BIKEWAY (8.25 miles), B–F, City of Philadelphia, Fairmount Park Commission.

New Jersey: PALISADES LONG PATH (11 miles), F, Palisades Interstate Park Commission.

New Jersey: PALISADES SHORE TRAIL (11.25 miles), F, Palisades Interstate Park Commission.

New York: HARRIMAN LONG PATH (16 miles), F, Palisades Interstate Park Commission.

We've been talking about all those things which seem interesting to us just to start your imagination working so you might begin thinking about what would interest you.

Now that you've got some ideas about that, how do you find out where to find your fun?

**Specific suggestions for picking an area:**

• Keep a clipping file of newspapers and magazine stories telling about activities and points of interest within easy traveling radius of your area.

• Go to automobile dealers and a gas station and ask for maps showing points of interest and activities within the state or a smaller area.

• Read what the encyclopedia says about your state and neighboring states. Consult guidebooks in the library.

• Ask large city newspapers if they have pamphlets describing studies they may have done for recreational purposes.

• Write to the Chamber of Commerce of counties (including your own) within your limited traveling radius.

• Write to the agency that handles recreational inquiries for each state within your traveling radius. Address your inquiry to: Travel Director or Parks and Recreation Commissioner, Capital City, Name of State, and even if the state government has no such office you can be sure that your query will be channeled to the proper department.

• For information about national forests write to: Forest Service, U.S. Department of Agriculture, Washington, D.C. 20240.

• For information about national parks write to: National Park Service, U.S. Department of the Interior, Washington, D.C. 20240.

• For information about Canada write to: Canadian Government Travel Bureau, Ottawa, Ontario, Canada.

• For information about Mexico write to: Mexican Government Tourism, Suite 3508, 630 Fifth Avenue, New York, New York 10019.

When writing for information, ask for general literature telling what recreational activities are available in the area in which you are interested, and also give a short list of your specific interests, because they just may have something on that subject they would be glad to send you. Tell them, too, if you have any physical handicaps so they can advise you of campgrounds or trails that have been specially designed to make your trip more enjoyable.

• Send for any of the following government pamphlets and books that might lead you to interesting adventure:

*Hiking and Hiking Trails, A Trails and Trail-Based Activities Bibliography* can be purchased from the National Technical Information Service, Springfield, Va. 22151, for $3.00.

A bibliography on bicycling and bicycling trails will soon be published and should be available from the above or from the Superintendent of Documents.

The following are all available from the Superintendent of

Documents, U.S. Government Printing Office, Washington, D.C. 20402:

*American Indian Calendar* (30¢) lists Indian celebrations, rodeos, etc. that take place annually in 24 states.

*Back-Country Travel in the National Park System* (35¢); stock number 2405–02–67.

*Boating Regulations in the National Park System* (30¢); catalogue number I29.9:B63/970

*Fishing in the National Park System* (30¢) lists all fishing areas, types of fishing available and license requirements for anglers in national park areas; catalogue number I29.2:F53/3/969.

*Living History in the National Park System* (30¢) describes live demonstrations of historic equipment and techniques which can be seen by park visitors; catalogue number I29.2:L76.

*National Parks and Landmarks* (55¢) lists and briefly describes all areas administered by the National Park Service and designated landmarks of national significance; catalogue number I29.66:970.

*National Parks of the United States* ($1.50), a series of eight maps showing the National Park System; catalogue number I29.6:P23.

*Room to Roam* (75¢), a guidebook listing more than 400 unusual places for travel adventure.

*Vacationing with the Indians* (30¢) gives Indian reservation camping information.

*Winter Activities in the National Park System* (35¢) lists winter recreation facilities and programs at 12 National Park System areas from Maine to California; catalogue number I29.2:AC8.

Once you've got a little camping experience under your belt, and if you have a little spare cash on hand, you might want to take advantage of one of the airlines' fly-and-camp programs. Pick a destination, keep your supplies to a minimum so you can carry most of your needs with you on the plane, then either use one of the camper vehicles that have a tie-in with the airline or arrange to rent a station wagon, small van or whatever best suits your needs through an independent agency. (Phone your local airline information office for up-to-date details.) You could have a very super-special kind of a weekend, letting you do the kind of camping you always wanted to do no matter where, even though you have only two or three days. The possibilities boggle the mind. For instance:

• You and some friends might fly from inland states to New England, camp near a fishing village and make and glut yourselves on a real New England clambake.

• You might camp in the area of your grandparents' or great-grandparents' old homestead and dig into family history. On a camping trip that we once took in Colorado, we had a delightful time tracking down Inez's grandfather's homestead. Hillary Harris was his name and he had been a pioneer doctor near Kremmling, which is just over the Continental Divide west of Denver in the high, high Rockies. We started with a letter to the Colorado Historical Society long before we left home and wound up having a cookout on a mountainside with Butch and Jan de Berard, who now own the old homestead. Inez recognized it, by the way, by the shape of a nearby canyon which her mother as a young girl had reproduced in an oil painting which had hung on their living room wall in California during the years Inez was growing up.

Although this was not a weekend fly-and-camp trip it could have been, because we only spent two days in the Kremmling area and we think the idea is just too good not to pass on to others.

There's one thing that would have to be different about a fly-and-camp trip from the one- or two-night, close-to-home camping trips we've been discussing up to now and this is it: Make reservations for the flight, campground space, recvee and special events you might like to attend well ahead of time.

Some travel agencies can make the arrangements for you and might even have some suggestions for different types of activities you might like to try at the other end of a flight. And don't forget that helpful old standby, the local Chamber of Commerce.

What we've been trying to say is that overnight and weekend camping can be the perfect way of opening new horizons, of finding new adventure, of getting to know nature, of rediscovering history, of learning about the land around you and all the people who inhabit it. All this (unless you choose to fly and camp) at bargain rates and without once visiting Yosemite, Yellowstone or other overpublicized places.

So much so that keeping this in mind you and your family and friends may decide that weekend camping is definitely for all the time and not for once in a while. Travel south this week, north next week, then east, then west. Boundaries are no barrier. Cross them. Get to know the wonders all over. You need no passport to travel across state lines or to cross into Canada or Mexico. Go where the spirit moves you—if it's within that 200-mile radius we've mentioned.

More and more, campgrounds are being built near all types of recreational activities. You may be surprised to find out how many there are within a short drive from home.

### AFTER CHOOSING AN AREA, PICK A CAMPGROUND

Your choice of campgrounds is among three categories— commercial campgrounds operated for profit by private interests; improved and unimproved campgrounds operated by a branch of government including municipalities, counties, states or national, and the provinces in Canada. Let's look at each of the three.

**Commercial Campgrounds:** It is in one of these that you can expect to find most of the comforts of home. In exchange for a fee that may range from $2 to $5 a day, they'll provide you with a range of services and conveniences that may include electricity, sewage-dumping station, modern toilets and showers, coin-operated laundries, picnic tables, fireplaces, wood pile, garbage disposal and perhaps pickup, and water lines at each campsite. Some also may have swimming pools; some may be situated on natural waters suitable for both swimming and fishing; some waters may be large enough for boating and so the campground also would have a launching ramp.

Among the many other facilities that you may find in commercial campgrounds: ice-vending machines, grocery or general stores, bike rentals, playgrounds for people of all ages, teen centers, dance floors, little theaters, museums, lending libraries.

There are quite a number of commercial campgrounds that have tents already set up and rent them along with the campsite. Some rent camping trailers with the site, and if you become attached to it during your stay you can buy it and pull it home, applying part of the cost of rental to the purchase price!

In short, you name it; somewhere in this vast land of ours you'll find a commercial campground that's got it. The scope of the facilities will determine whether you pay closer to $2 a day or $5 a day for the privilege of camping there— oh yes, plus 50 cents a head per day if there are more than four people in your party.

**Improved Public Campgrounds:** Just as the word "public" implies, these are campgrounds owned, operated and supervised by a government agency. Usually that agency will be on either the state or federal level, but more and more municipalities and counties around the country are getting into the camping act.

Improvements at these public Edens often don't begin to approach those to be found at private campgrounds that are run for profit. Rather, they sometimes are nothing more than a fireplace, picnic table, garbage can, pit toilet and similar essentials. Facilities vary from camp to camp, however, and many public campgrounds boast such up-to-date facilities as flush toilets, hot showers and so forth—but often at more modest prices and definitely in more pleasing settings than most of the private campgrounds.

Commercial campgrounds are more likely to be close to well-traveled highways; some operators won't hesitate to chop down a tree or a grove of them to make room for a plastic swimming pool or another campsite. Not so, however, at campgrounds that are run by and for you, the people.

There the settings definitely are more apt to be wooded, rustic, picturesque and as close to being the way nature meant the land to be as civilization will permit in this age of what politicians and profiteers like to call "progress."

Not quite so rustic and certainly not so improved are the rest areas that are to be found every 50 miles or so along many of the highways that crisscross both the United States and Canada. We mention this because in many states one-night camping is permitted in these rest areas—a fact that you may well bear in mind the next time you plan a weekend camping trip and for one reason or another have no particular destination in mind.

**Unimproved Public Campgrounds:** It is at these campgrounds that you get the most that you possibly can out of a weekend camping trip, because the name means just what it says: very few improvements beyond the natural state. But, oh, what a lovely state that usually is! Here you are most likely to see nature as it was meant to be seen. Civilized facilities are virtually nil, consisting essentially of nothing more than a place to park, a crude fireplace and a garbage can.

By their very nature, unimproved campgrounds usually are located on seldom-traveled back roads or trails that thread through landscape that still is pretty much untouched by man. The scenery is magnificent, the smell of sage or pine is breathtaking, the feeling of being in truly primitive and wild country is no farther than a few steps from camp.

Some campgrounds accept reservations (most private ones do), some operate on a first-come, first-served basis. Some popular public campgrounds are reserved for the entire summer season a few days after they start taking reservations, which may be many months in advance. Since you probably won't be going a very expensive toll call away from home for your midweek camping, you may want to phone the campground of your choice even if it's the off season, just to be sure a convention of some kind has not booked its facilities or it's not crowded for some other reason. If you're going camping on a weekend or in the summer, you may be willing to take a chance if you're sure the campground is underused, but it's always best to phone or make a reservation by mail as far ahead as you can.

You will be able to take your dog (or other family pet) to many privately owned campgrounds and to some of the public ones, but both types of campground will most likely insist that the pet be kept on a leash and may require proof of rabies inoculation.

Also, if you don't look your age, be prepared to prove that you're eighteen or over.

Opening and closing dates vary and usually are in May and October, but more and more campgrounds are staying open all year, though sometimes only for weekends during the coldest winter months.

How do you find out all of these things about specific campgrounds as well as their names and addresses?

The easiest way to get a lot of capsulized information is to consult a copy of either the American Automobile Association's *Camping & Trailering Guide,* published annually on a regional basis and free to members; or either Rand McNally's *Guidebook to Campgrounds* or Woodall's *Trailer and Camping Guide,* both of which are sold in camping-goods stores and may be seen in your local library. These three publications, by the way, list both commercial and public campgrounds, so it's a good idea to have at least one of them if you intend to do much camping. They are updated annually but there is no need to invest in a new one every year. To give you an idea of the scope of the information to be found in these books, Rand McNally's *Guidebook to Campgrounds,* for instance, includes a map for each state with reference numbers showing where the campgrounds, both public and private, are located. Then there is a listing of those campgrounds, showing the following things: size, cleanliness, rating, access roads and distance from closest town, number of tentsites, minimum fee, season, time limit and whether or not pets are permitted. A rundown is given of such conveniences as trailer space, tables, firewood, kitchen shelter, shelters, change house, flush toilets, showers, ice, laundry, café-snack

bar, drinking water, store, hiking, trails, swimming, fishing, boating, playground, golf, riding, archery, boat rental and launching ramp and other information.

Then, since the guidebooks list the post-office address for each campground, you can write for more detailed information about those in the area which you have chosen to visit.

Besides information about campgrounds, the guidebooks also have a handy listing (they don't all carry the same information, so you might find it a good idea, as we do, to have more than one) of the regulations governing traveling in each state, and such things as: speed limits, trailer size limits, whether or not passengers are permitted in trailer or camper, highways on which trailers are not allowed, and which bridges and tunnels have regulations about bottled gas and what they are.

Additionally, they may tell you if camping is permitted in a state's (or Canadian province's) roadside rest areas and if, where and under what circumstances overnight off-roadway parking is allowed.

Besides consulting the guidebooks, there are many other

ways of learning the locations and facilities of campgrounds. Among them:

• Write to the U.S. Department of the Interior, Washington, D.C. 20240, and ask for a list of federally operated campgrounds, their facilities and regulations, in the state in which you would like to sojourn.

• Write to the Superintendent of Documents, U.S. Government Printing Office, Washington, D.C. 20402, for the pamphlet *Camping in the National Park System* (30¢), which lists all campgrounds operated on national parklands; catalogue number I29.71:971.

• See also the listing of places to write and pamphlets to write for under the heading "Specific Suggestions for Picking an Area."

• Attend a camping or outdoor show if there is one near you. They are usually held in the early spring in metropolitan areas. And you can fill a couple of shopping bags full of literature, much of it about facilities within 200 miles of your home. Not only will there be campground literature, there will be people there to answer questions.

• Backpackers will find U.S. Geological Survey maps invaluable in helping them locate suitable campsites close to a source of water. For maps of areas east of the Mississippi, write The Director, U.S. Geological Survey, Washington, D.C. For maps of areas west of the Mississippi, the address is Denver Federal Center, Denver, Colorado.

*Before paying an entrance fee to any national park, monument, historic site, battlefield or other national recreation area, check with the attendant to see if you can save money by purchasing a $10 Golden Eagle pass.*


## Finding Your Own Private Campground

It's still possible (much more so in some areas than others, obviously) to find your own private campground. Take some exploratory rides (off the throughways, of course), staying within 50 miles of home port and keeping an eye open for places that look right for a one-night camping excursion. If you find a spot, ask permission to use it.

One of the best such spots is a farm where the owner might be glad to have you stay for a small fee.

Maybe you have a friend who has some acreage in the country and would let you use it for a night if you did a good job of policing it before leaving. He might even decide to go with you! If it's close enough, you might make it a hiking or bicycling expedition.

Maybe you could take a tip from our nephew and niece, Harry and Diane Bloksberg, who live in Massachusetts. They have seven children, but that doesn't faze them. Diane has a sister who lives in Maine and has lots of land. Harry and Diane have a two-room cottage tent that measures 10 feet by 16 feet, and every summer they keep it pitched and ready for use on the Maine homestead. Come Friday night, they pile the kids, groceries, camp stove and blankets into their station wagon, drive to Maine, and on Sunday night they are home again.

## Campsites for Sale

More and more areas are being devoted to the type of campground where each camper owns his own site. You will find salesmen with their maps at the camp shows, and on paper they look very enticing. If you buy a campsite, when you're ready to go camping for a weekend you'll have no worries about finding a place to pitch your tent or park your trailer. Some sites are undoubtedly excellent, but some will probably turn out to be something like setting up housekeeping in a supermarket parking lot, so we'd highly recommend you go see before signing on the dotted line no matter how the salesman tries to convince you the last tree is about to be taken. Some of the things you should check:

• Can you use the site for all or at least most of the year?

• Is water readily available to your site or is it in a well on the other side of the development? Maybe a well that hasn't been dug?

• Are the sanitary facilities indefinite and how far are they from the site you are considering?

• What about drainage?

• The development site may look like lovely wilderness now, but how will it be when it's carved up into (how many?) campsites and filled with people and vehicles?

• What surrounds the campground? Maybe a future supermarket and housing development will replace those lovely old oaks before too many years have passed!

• Will there be things to do in the immediate vicinity if you do decide to buy—swimming, fishing, boating, exploring, hiking, etc.?

If you are thinking of buying a campsite, you might better consider buying several acres all your own. If you look long enough, you may be able to do so without spending much money. But you should ask yourself the same questions as listed above and many more. You want to be sure you have access to your site, that the title is clear, that you have either water on your land or easy access to water. Are there natural hazards that will make it difficult for your children to play freely? How much does the temperature fluctuate? Would flash floods temporarily and swiftly drown your property? Are there any plans for building dams or super highways that would spoil (or maybe add to) the value of the land as a campsite? Is it too much of a wilderness site for your knowledge and physical and mechanical ability to cope with? Are there any area zoning laws that might interfere with your plans?

If you are willing to go to the trouble of checking this list of questions and many more that we haven't thought of, there are several ways we can suggest to go about looking for some land, chief among them being to use your imagination and ingenuity:

• Check ads in camping magazines.

• Check the real-estate ads in the nearest city newspaper, looking especially for listings of catalogues you can send for that show available farmlands.

• Check with real-estate agents in areas where you would like to buy.

• Write to the Superintendent of Documents, Government Printing Office, Washington, D.C., 20402, and subscribe to *Our Public Land,* a Department of the Interior quarterly; cost, $1.00. You may find something you will want to bid on.

• Check with Chambers of Commerce in the areas that interest you to see if there are any logging companies with holdings there. Sometimes you can lease very nice land from them at a reasonable price.

• Check with state departments of agriculture.

• Do your weekend camping in the general area where you would like to buy campsite acreage. Nose around for for-sale signs, get to know local people and feel them out about land that may be for sale.

And we wish you good luck in your search because we feel that the more people who buy acreage to use for camping, the better, because they will keep it relatively unspoiled and safe from the concrete pourers and other exploiters. Although the acreage you buy may be small, if thousands of others do the same, it can add up to quite a bundle. Why not interest friends in acquiring adjoining parcels of land with the same thing in mind?

## A Word of Caution

To conclude this chapter on "When and Where to Go," let us caution you: If you're a greenhorn at the game, camp only when and where you know the weather and travel conditions will be moderate. For the very rugged, the physically fit man and woman, boy and girl, there's a lot of wild country and wild rivers to explore, and in just about every one of the 50 states. But don't make your first few weekend camping trips extremes, such as hot desert or cold wilderness. Or for that matter, any kind of wilderness until you really know the camping score or have a knowledgeable professional guide to lead you, or go with a group who know what they're doing.

How do you find a knowledgeable guide or group you can accompany? One way is to ask a good camping outfitter to recommend a guide. Some outfitters are guides themselves or have guides who work with them and arrange wilderness trips. If you don't know a reputable outfitter, check with your local Chamber of Commerce or recreation department or the Chamber of Commerce in the area where you hope to go mountain climbing or whatever. You can also check with your local Chamber of Commerce or recreation department to see if there is a local chapter of such nonprofit organizations as the National Campers and Hikers Association (or write that particular organization's headquarters at 7172 Transit Road, Buffalo, New York 14221) and explore the possibility of becoming a member of one of their groups, or ask their advice about other groups you can contact. The NCHA and similar clubs often have displays and representatives at outdoor and camping shows.

There are also such organizations as the following you can join:

*The American Forestry Association,* 1319 18th St. N.W., Washington, D.C. 20036; *The American Youth Hostels,* 20 West 17th St., Dept. M, New York, N.Y. 10011 (their summer program includes camping, canoeing, cycling, hiking); *The Appalachian Mountain Club,* 5 Joy St., Boston, Mass. 02108 (canoeing, backpacking, outings, etc., camping by day, week or longer); *The Sierra Club,* 1050 Mills Tower, San Francisco, Calif. 94104 (besides wilderness outings, has local walking, knapsack and camping trips nearly every weekend); *The Wilderness Society,* 729 15th St. N.W., Washington, D.C. 20005 (with horseback riding, hiking, backpacking, canoeing trips open to everyone).

Such camping and hiking organizations are usually conservation-oriented, and your membership dues will help pay for literature they send to keep you informed of developments and, hopefully, active in supporting their programs. Of course, you should evaluate the programs proposed by any club you join and be sure they are genuinely designed to protect and preserve our great out-of-doors and are based on thorough exploration and study. These genuine and worthwhile concerns not only deserve but *must have* your active support if there is to be the kind of escape from the tensions of the cities into our national parks and wilderness country available to us all—camping grounds of a quality that will provide us with the benefits we all desperately need.

You don't have to wait until you join a club to start doing your part. Watching television and reading newspapers and magazines will give you enough information to begin.

Actively support public officials who initiate and support

worthwhile conservation measures. Let them know your opinions on issues as they arise, by word of mouth, letter and telegram. (If you don't know who the officials are who represent you or how to reach them, look up the League of Women Voters in your local telephone directory, phone them and they will give you all the information you need.)

If you want to be able to have a say in what's being done to preserve your right and opportunity for pleasant camping, that is what you must do. More than that, that is what you must do to preserve the quality of your home environment— and probably life itself for your grandchildren.

# PART II

# Getting Ready to Go Camping

# Chapter 1

## Wheeled Camping Vehicles

Come summertime, visit any campground in the country and you'll see camping vehicles of every conceivable type, size and description.

Or if you don't want to travel that far just to look at the large variety of what the camping industry calls "recreational vehicles"—recvees for short—and let your fingers do the traveling through the yellow pages of the phone book. Then pay a visit to the showrooms and the show yards of the dealers near you.

Don't stop with one visit to just one dealer, though. Look over the full line of recvees carefully. Compare the wares of the scores of different manufacturers. Check the many built-in conveniences that all of them offer in their models.

Look. Look. Look. And come away convinced that all of them are good. Convinced but confused, because they're all so good that you can't for the life of you decide which one would be best for you.

So right here and now is the place for us to give you our opinion, to wit: The best possible vehicle for you may very

well be the automobile or station wagon that you already own and drive every day. In other words, you don't need a recreational vehicle in order to enjoy yourself, particularly if you are a beginning weekend camper.

The time to acquire a recvee, if ever, is after you've been on several overnight camping trips and have come in contact with other, more experienced campers in formal campgrounds; after you've seen their recreational vehicles up close, seen the specialties and the shortcomings of each that make them good or bad in given situations; after you've graduated to longer camping trips; after you've discovered what kind of terrain you prefer the most.

The choice of terrain is as wide as the North American continent is big: wild-river wilderness, low desert, high desert, mountaintop, forest, prairie, warm southern meadow, cold northern snowcap, by-boat-only island, junglelike bayou country or lush, plush private campground complete with every possible convenience necessary to make roughing it the softest vacation you've ever had.

After you've gone through all that is the time to determine what kind of recreational vehicle best suits your taste for outdoor living, outdoor adventure. For example, if you've decided that mountain camping is for you, you certainly wouldn't, or shouldn't, want to navigate a trailer up those rugged roads and around those rock-strewn switchbacks.

As we said, on your initial motor camping trips the vehicle to use is the car or station wagon you already own. And who knows? When the time comes to make a choice, you may very well decide that what you have now will do just fine.

That's what we learned and it took nothing more than a seven-week, 19-state, 6,000-mile camping trip to teach us. A trip, mind you, that took us over every possible kind of road from New York's Grand Central Parkway to 11,000-foot passes in the Colorado Rockies and unpaved, unimproved switchbacks in New Mexico's Sangre de Cristo Mountains.

Our vehicle? The family sedan, a two-door, six-cylinder Plymouth Valiant (which is an undersized car) to which we added only heavy-duty shocks and a removable roof rack.

We packed everything with us—complete camping equipment including such bulky things as stove, lamp, heater and a six-week supply of fuel for all of them; tent, food staples and seasonings, cooler, cooking and eating utensils; bedding, toilet, several changes of clothing, fishing tackle for two, all the tools of a writer's trade including a portable typewriter, laundry supplies, camp chairs and folding table. We filled every inch of cargo space, not only on the roof rack and in the trunk, but in the back seat, too.

And what trouble did we encounter with our Valiant on that 6,000-mile, seven-week trip over every conceivable kind of road? Not even a flat tire.

Oh, yes! We did scrape a hole in our gas tank while negotiating a rock-pocked switchback in the hills overlooking the crossroads town of Arroyo Hondo, New Mexico. What trouble did it cause? We hightailed it back to the crossroads service station before our gas leaked away, and Abel Chacon, the owner-mechanic there, patched it up with a cake of brown laundry soap, sandpaper and a bit of liquid aluminum that he pressed out of a tube. How much did it cost? Five dollars and 40 cents and we kept the tube of liquid aluminum.

That same Plymouth Valiant is still our only family car as this book is being written two years later and we haven't had need, not even once, to give that tube another squeeze.

That's why we urge you to think twice before investing money in a recreational vehicle that you may use four or five weeks a year at the most, or if you are going to be strictly a weekend camper, perhaps not at all.

If you still want to shop around—go about it much as you would for any family car: start, as we said, by consulting the yellow pages and looking first under the heading "Campers and Travel Trailers." Then go look, compare, ask questions. And when you think you've made up your mind, still don't buy. Rent. Most recvee dealers rent as well as sell and many of them will apply the rental fee to the purchase price.

In other words, test-use the recreational vehicle of your choice on a weekend camping trip before you buy. Then if need be, rent another. And another.

When you've tried them all, you may decide that it's to your advantage not to buy but only to rent whenever you go camping. Where, for instance, if you live in a big city, will you park your recvee when not in use?

So, with all of those cautionary preliminaries out of the way, here is a rundown of the various kinds of recreational vehicles to be found in the great American market place.

**Pickup Covers:** Of the many types of recreational vehicles we see on the road today, we don't know which came first. However, we suspect that it was the boxlike cover that graces the back of so many pickup trucks from coast to coast and particularly in the mountain states.

Some covers are called shells, others are called caps. Shells are usually nothing more than a cab-high box made of aluminum, wood, steel, fiberglass or a combination thereof and having station-wagon type rear doors. The cap usually is more elaborate, some of them eight to ten inches higher than the cab, with insulated walls, windows and walk-in rear door. The shells, as the word implies, have nothing whatsoever built into their interiors while the caps may or may not come with full-length side benches that double as bunks. More than that is up to you. Pay the price and you'll find someone to build in almost anything you want even if extras have to be hung from the ceiling.

What do we think of such pickup covers? The answer is this: quite highly.

In fact, if ever the day should come that we decide we need a recvee for camping, we'd buy a pickup truck with an insulated, windowed cap which would be fitted out with nothing more than bunks. The cost of such a cap would be considerably less than $500. All the rest of the camping equipment we'd require, whether for two days or two months, could easily be carried in the truck bed—in other words, inside the cover. When in camp we'd rig the outside with a dining fly or station-wagon type snap-on tent and more than that we'd never need.

Covers are made to fit all sizes of pickup trucks from the

smallest Japanese-made to the largest turned out by American manufacturers.

**Pickup Truck Camper:** This is a cover with class. The class is provided by a couple of feet of added height, an overhang over the cab that serves as a bed, sometimes an aft-end extension to add space, and an interior fitted out with all the comforts of home—or at least as many of them as you feel you want on a camping trip.

Depending upon the make and model and whether you want to pay a thousand dollars or several thousand dollars, campers can sleep from two to six. Some have full kitchens and some have not; some have toilets and showers and some do not; some have ladders to a rooftop sundeck; some have rooftop boat racks; some slide into the truck bed, some are chassis-mounted.

But remember this: The money you pay for a camper does not include the pickup truck you'll need. Add the cost of the two of them together and you'll see that what you're buying calls for a tidy outlay. So, since you're spending all that money, perhaps you'll decide to buy a motor home or a camper van. Both types offer models in the $5,000 to $8,000 price range.

Let's hasten to say right here and now that you need not spend all that money on an elaborately tailored and outfitted camper. The less expensive, less luxuriously turned-out models will do just as well, particularly on a weekend camping trip, and no matter how many there are in your party.

Truck campers are good. They're practical too, particularly if you do your over-the-road camping in terrain that's made to order for them. We say that because truck campers also have their shortcomings—all that height on the back of your pickup can act like a sail in a high wind, and you'd better beware of low-hanging wires and tree branches. Not only that, but they also can be unwieldy in rough mountain country and on sidehills.

These major truck camper faults are inherent in the vehicle because the bulk of its weight is too high. However, at least two manufacturers have introduced variations that provide cover roadability with camper comfort.

Let's look at them one at a time:

*Pop-Top Camper:* On the road this looks like a camper cover. Popped up in camp, it looks like a truck camper but without the cab overhang. The change is not done with mirrors, but rather with a hydraulic system that pops the shell upward from a four-foot six-and-a-half-inch exterior height when lowered to an interior height of six feet three inches when raised. The cost of a ten-foot-long pop-topper that's made of steel-reinforced and weather-insulated fiberglass as of the time this is being written is $2,795 (plus truck, of course). It sleeps two as is but can be tailored to accommodate more.

*Pullman Camper:* Here again, on the road this pickup truck recvee looks like a camper cover. But in camp, lo, what a difference—not upward but rearward. It's done with the touch of a finger that activates Teflon rollers on which a steel rooftop canopy rides out to double the cover's length. The interior of the cover is rigged out with folding bunks that will sleep three. With the canopy pulled out and a canvas curtain (optional) set into place by means of a rope slot, it will sleep that many more if need be—besides, of course, providing plenty of room for cooking and dining. The cost as of this writing: $1,095 (plus truck).

**Camper or Tent Trailers:** Every year, come summertime, you see more and more of them on the road, rectangular little trailers that look like a box on wheels but open up into a tent containing just about everything anyone would want or need for a camping vacation.

Folded down and ready for the road, they stand about three feet from ground to roof. Their other dimensions range from seven feet by four feet to seven feet by fourteen feet. In camp, with the turn of a crank or a few minutes of manual labor, they burst forth like a rose into a complete canvas-side living unit that stands more or less firm on four corner jacks.

Most have hard plastic tops, some have canvas tops, one is being marketed now that has upward-telescoping plastic sides. In full bloom, their headroom measures upward of six feet. Most have winged platforms on either end that serve as double bunks.

Depending upon the model, these campers will sleep from two to eight, have dining tables and upholstered benches that serve also as bunks; stoves, sinks, toilets and much storage space.

These units are so light that in tight spots they can easily be unhitched and maneuvered around by hand. Their tongue weight: no more than 150 pounds. They trailer nicely, much more so than the larger travel trailers, but like all trailers they do have their unavoidable problems—sometimes a bit of a yaw when underway for instance. Additionally, if they are not built snugly enough, their boxed-down interiors can and will gather road dust and dirt, and all those moving parts which enable them to be raised and lowered can be whacked out of kilter.

Still, if it's a trailer that you think you must have in order to enjoy a camping weekend, we think that a camper trailer is your best buy. Their cost: anywhere from about $600 to about $3,000.

*Trailer Hitches.* We could write reams on this highly important subject, but when we were done you probably would say, "My gosh, I'd better have this put on by an expert." We won't waste the space beyond this quick word: All hitches for camper, travel and boat trailer should be bolted or riveted to the frame of your pulling vehicle and that is a job that should be done only by professionals. The people who sell you a trailer may make the hitch installation for you; if not, they probably can recommend someone who will; or see your own automobile mechanic.

When the installation is completed, by all means insist that the trailer salesman show you in painstaking, specific detail (1) how it hooks up, (2) how the brakes and lights attach to the pulling vehicle, (3) how and where the safety chain attaches, (4) how much air pressure both your trailer and vehicle tires should carry.

And then take the whole kit and kaboodle to your garage and have the mechanic double-check everything.

**Van Campers:** As we wrote this chapter, there arrived in the mail the May 1972 issue of *Camping Guide* and in it there is an article on van campers by Brent and Sandy Salmon, a team who know whereof they write.

Wasting no time in getting to the reason for their piece, they say in the first paragraph that the growth in van-truck popularity "has been phenomenal and is due, no doubt, to the fact that the van is truly a double-duty vehicle."

And in the second paragraph they add this: "It can be used to haul a Scout troop one day, materials for a do-it-yourself project another and be a very acceptable shopping vehicle the next."

To which we add the fact that more and more vans are being driven by the under-thirty generation than ever before, not only for camping and for getting around the country, but also for doing such simple everyday things as driving to campus or the nearest rock festival.

Stripped down to its skeleton, a van camper is a van truck just as it came from the factory. It might be used, as the Salmons suggested, during the work week by a carpenter, plumber or painter to go about his business. Then, come the weekend, if it's scouting that he is interested in, it can be used to take Boy Scouts or Girl Scouts, Cubs or Brownies on an overnight camping trip.

And so apparently from such beginnings came a light to the automotive industry. If a van truck could do so well for a Scout troop on a Saturday and Sunday, then obviously it also could be converted for family camping use, not only on weekends but on any of the 365 days of the year. All this, while also serving for business, trade or shopping whenever not in service as a recreational vehicle.

It all depends upon the type of conversion that is made.

Did the idea catch on? We will tell you this: The automakers do not handle the conversions. That chore is left to others, and today there are more than 50 companies that specialize in converting vans turned out by Dodge, Ford, Chevrolet, GMC and Volkswagen into van campers.

Like anything else available to the buying public, what you get is what you pay for. Prices of the package, depending upon the size and the make of the truck and the elaborateness of the conversion, will range from about $4,000 to about $9,500.

Camping vans in the upper price brackets, what with their higher roofs, extended lengths and all-the-comforts-of-home interior appointments, are reaching out of the camper class and into the realm of motor homes. And that's a fact backed up by the camper van's variety of other names, among them: mini home, micro home, maxi van, maxi wagon, bus.

But no matter what camper van you choose, no matter by what name it is called, you will have bought yourself quite a bit of get-up-and-go camping (or living) vehicle. And, we hope, one to fill all your needs, not only for today but for many more years to come.

What with five major van-truck manufacturers turning out several models every year and 50 or more companies each with a variety of plans for their conversion into van campers, we'd advise that you do an awful lot of shopping around before buying. More so than with any other type of recreational vehicle.

Do you want a six- or an eight-cylinder engine? Do you want a light or a high-gross vehicle weight van? Do you want swinging side doors, sliding side doors or no side doors at all? And how about side windows? Do you want swivel seats or fixed seats? How do they ride empty? How do they ride with full load? Do you want a fixed extended top or one that rides up and down by manual crank? What is the center of gravity? Are there two people in your family or eight? Do you want a hookup that permits the pitching and the attaching of a tent when in camp? Will you be traveling smooth-paved parkways or rutted dirt roads?

All this will give you an idea of the many questions you should have answers to before putting your signature to a contract for the purchase of a van camper.

That, so far as we are concerned, completes this book's rundown of automotive recreational vehicles. And for good and sufficient reason: We think that is all the worthy-of-the-name recreational vehicles there are. Manufacturers of motor homes, mobile homes and travel trailers may argue with us, but the fact remains that we don't now and never will consider them vehicles in which to go camping. Certainly not when they are priced in the five-figure bracket, certainly not when some of them run as high as $30,000. To us, "going camping" in one of those would be somewhat equivalent to

having house movers tow our seven-room home in Long
Beach, New York, from campsite to campsite across the
country.

However, though we are done with conventional recvees,
we are not done with this chapter because we know of at
least four variations that are worthy of note and which
we cannot fit into any particular category, and there are at
least two other vehicles which certainly could be used and
are being used for getting to and from campsites: bicycles
and motorcycles.

To us, they are just as much recreational vehicles as truck
campers, van campers, camper trailers and such. So let's get
with it, beginning with the newest vehicle to hit the American camping scene. It's called:

**Playpac:** Until the spring camping shows of 1972 rolled
around nobody we know had ever seen or heard of one. Then
in the summer of 1972 they began to appear on the nation's
highways, in tow behind the smallest cars ever made, both
foreign and domestic.

So what is a Playpac? A Playpac is a 990-pound two-
wheeled trailer made of unitized fiberglass that's meant
specifically for small-car owners, yet can be towed just as
well by the biggest car ever made.

Except for a couple of fore and aft V-shaped dimensions,
in appearance the Playpac is a two-wheel mounted box that
measures 7 feet 4 inches from ground to dome, 13 feet 3
inches from rear bumper to end of hitch, and 7 feet in width.
But more important to campers than such exterior dimensions, its interior headroom is 6 feet 1 inch, its interior length
10 feet 3½ inches.

In that space is built a two-burner stove, 35-pound icebox,
sink, toilet, water tank, heater, bunks for four, dining table
and miscellaneous decorator and engineer items. The price:
$1,795.

If you drive a small car and if you're allergic to pitching a
tent, we suggest that you look this new item over the next
time you're caught in the rain on a weekend camping trip.

We said earlier in this chapter that the best possible vehicle to use on a weekend camping trip is the car that you

already own. And here are three automotive additions to prove it. One we call an "auto-top tent," another a "car camper," the third a "driveaway camper." To be honest with you, we've never seen any of them in use nor have we run into them at shows. But we've read ads and seen pictures of the first two in camping and outdoor magazines, and the third was recommended to us by Jim Bashline, Dan's fellow member in the Outdoor Writers Association of America, and they all merit looking into.

**Auto-Top Tent:** The manufacturers, the Camp'otel Corporation of Fort Worth, Texas, don't call it that. "Car Camper" is the name they give it. However, we prefer auto-top tent because that is exactly what it is, and we don't want you to confuse it with the other campers that we write about in this book.

The auto-top is a large rectangular box that rides on top of almost any car or station wagon from Volkswagen to Cadillac and, although only ten inches high, carries in it four foam mattresses, bedding and other gear for four; stove; food; cooking and eating utensils including sink, table and benches; bathroom-dressing room complete with shower and toilet; and dining fly. There is also a ladder for climbing up and down because with a couple of simple maneuvers that box also blossoms into a tent up there on the roof of the car or station wagon. As for the cooking, dining and bathroom areas, they set up on the ground behind or alongside the vehicle.

And there you are, high and dry no matter what the weather. The price according to an ad in the June 1972 issue of *Camping Guide:* $329 for the sleeping-dining outfit; under $490 with all options, plus shipping. The place to write for free literature: Camp'otel Corporation, 2822 West Lancaster, Fort Worth, Texas 76107.

**Car Camper:** This unique fiberglass unit, shaped like the letter L lying on its side, is attached to the family automobile by removing the trunk lid so that the bottom of the L can fit into the trunk while the long arm of the L (only 14 inches thick) extends over the roof of the car where it is held down by clamps attached to the rain gutters.

So installed, you are ready for the road. In camp, four

spring-loaded corner braces pop up foldaway canvas sides to a height of six feet two inches complete with sleeping facilities for four, stove, sink, dining area and plenty of storage space. Total weight: 350 pounds. Price as of June 1972: $1,190. Its manufacturer: Tripper Industries.

**Driveaway Camper:** This is the one that Jim Bashline told us about. It is called a "top-pac camper" because in transit, it is carried in a box atop the car (just like the auto-top tent), and in camp you lower the four long legs on which it stands, drive out from under, and have your car to do with what you will while your camp stays put.

Here's what Jim had to say about it in his letter to us:

It weighs just 250 pounds, rides on top of the family car and sleeps four comfortably. [It] is all aluminum construction and is carried on regular steel carriers. Folded, the unit measures 6' x 8' x 10". Erected, it is an 8' x 12' x 7' cabin with enough headroom to accommodate the over six-footers.

Now—get this! Enclosed in the package, all neatly stowed away, are two double-decker bunks, an aluminum table with four chairs, propane stove, snap-in vinyl floor, two screened windows, a storm door with lock, and storm windows for all.

The price as of the date of Jim's letter: $695. The distributors: Gyrfalcon Inc., 1104 Fernwood Avenue, Camp Hill, Penn. 17011.

**Motorcycles:** We're not suggesting that you rush right out and buy one, but a motorcycle is a wonderful little vehicle to use on a two- or three-day camping trip. It will get you where you want to go more quickly than anything else, it will scoot around just about any obstacle, it will negotiate any steep mountain trail, any rutted switchback, any kind of terrain you'll ever encounter.

The trick is to travel light. Just take along with you the gear that you would have on a walking trip, all of it nicely stowed away in a backpack (see Chapter 2, Part II). Lash it onto the so-called idiot seat; if you need anything more, pack it into saddlebags or panniers and away you go.

But, although you are on a motorcycle and can travel far, we urge you to plan your trip so that you arrive at your chosen campsite no later than noon; 10:00 A.M. is even better for good and sufficient reason: The less time you spend on the road, the more time you will have to enjoy camp life.

Or, if you must travel long distances, start earlier and still plan on being in camp by ten. Noon at the latest.

**Bicycles:** Under the heading "Motorcycles" we said that we do not suggest that you rush right out and buy one. But now we do. If you're not in good physical shape, buy a bicycle and whip yourself back to where you belong. If you are in good physical shape, buy a bike and stay that way.

And then, when you know that you are able to pedal anywhere from 5 to 50 miles in half a day, by all means use your bike for overnight camping trips.

A bicycle, we think, is the ideal wheeled vehicle. It's good exercise. It doesn't pollute the air. It will get you where you want to go, uphill or down, and let you really see the sights along the way. It poses no parking problems.

Distances of 5 to 50 miles in half a day are not difficult to travel—not with one of today's multispeed bikes. An experienced, physically fit rider should easily be able to pedal a three-speed bicycle 10 miles in an hour, a ten-speed bike 20 miles in an hour. So even 50 miles from home to campsite could allow you plenty of time in camp to do what you want to do.

When shopping for a bike, stick to the three- to ten-speeders because they handle like a fine car, while a one-speeder handles more like a truck. Semiballoon tires are best for all-purpose use and come-what-may terrain, and a low ratio gear range will help you to climb hills better.

Although there are both men's and women's bicycles on the market, the frame on women's bicycles will not stand up to use so long as will that on the men's.

Bikes range in height from 19 to 26 inches, and to determine which is best for you, straddle the frame and plant both

your feet flat on the ground. Then, if there is one or two
inches of clearance between you and the top bar, that is the
bike for you.

Collapsible bicycles have their advantages—namely, they
fold down into small packages and are easy to haul. But they
also have their disadvantages in that they handle too much
like a one-speed bicycle.

Pack your gear as you would for backpacking (see Chapter
2, Part II) and lash it firmly to a small piece of hardboard
that in turn is strapped to the rear-wheel carrier. There is
no need for the backpack frame, so you can leave that at
home. Anything more that you may find necessary to have
along for your camping trip can be carried in bags draped
over the handlebars, a front basket or rear-wheel panniers.

A three-speed bike should cost in the neighborhood of
$80, a ten-speed wheel closer to $100.

## Packing Your Gear

We won't say a word about packing your gear for an overnight camping trip in a recreational vehicle because every
one of them provides ample storage space for anything you'd
ever want to tote along, and every one of them stows differently.

But if your vehicle is either a station wagon or a family
sedan, we'd like to add a word about roof racks (or car carriers, as they are also called) if you can't fit all that you'll
require in wagon bed or auto trunk.

Roof racks are available both in automobile supply shops
and in most camping-goods stores, and they come in a variety
of sizes to fit any make or model of car or station wagon.
Their prices range from about $10 to about $25, but you
also can spend $50 and get yourself a covered carrier that
opens and closes like a clam shell and in which everything
will ride high and dry. Well, almost everything, because
there is a limit to what you can fit into a box.

As for the uncovered carrier, which clamps onto the car's
rain gutters, the sky's the limit as to what you can pack into
it. But we don't recommend that you go much more, if at all,

than six or eight inches above the rails. And only carry up there things that you know you will *not* need until you arrive in camp. Things that you *might* need along the way go into the trunk. Things that you *will* need go inside the car with you.

Don't pack anything loosely onto a roof rack. Rather, stow everything first in duffel bags, wooden boxes, suitcases or whatever, and then fit each of them in turn atop the rack. Stow the biggest items around the perimeter, the smaller bundles inside. But make sure that each of them straddles at least two of the cross bars so that they'll ride safely, securely, solidly.

Once everything is stowed in the roof rack, wrap it all with either the same grommet-fitted heavy-duty tarpaulin that you will use in camp or with specially fitted car carrier luggage covers that also are available. The latter are costly and we recommend that you stick with the one that can do double duty.

And now that everything is nicely covered, the next thing to do is tie it all down so it will stay put no matter at what speed you travel, nor how strong the wind. You can do that by wrapping it all, including the rack, with clothesline; just go round and round and round again a few more times with clothesline and then tie a secure knot, one that you learned in Boy Scouts.

Or you can be a lot more neat and efficient—and secure in the knowledge that your load will stay put—by also buying luggage grips that are made specifically for the purpose. The price: $2 to $5. They are made of six to eight lengths of extra-heavy elastic shock cord, all of them joined together on one end by a metal ring, each of them with a metal hook on the other end.

Just set the ring atop the center of your load, stretch each elastic cord to the outer rack bar—each at a different angle— and loop the hook over it. The elastic will set its own tension. Result: a tight-fitting spider that will hold your load firm like a fly in a web.

# Chapter 2

# Clothes, Sleeping Gear, Tarps, Tents, Backpacks, Toilets, and Miscellaneous Equipment

Until you have had some experience and can qualify as a competent judge of what you really need, for at least the first few camping trips you should try to get by with as little new equipment and clothes as possible. You may find that to do the simple kind of overnight and weekend camping we recommend for beginners, you don't need to buy anything, or at most only a few items.

There are essentially two kinds of camping—the kind in which you carry your food and extra clothes and all your gear on your back (backpacking) and the kind in which these things are carried for you (generally in a vehicle). There are shadings between. For instance, you can carry more on a horse or in a canoe than on your back, but as a rule neither the horse nor the canoe can carry so much as a car.

The weather may be both warm and cold on any given camping trip; obviously you should anticipate these variations in choosing clothing and equipment.

If you or any of your children might someday do more than one kind of camping and you're limited in funds, then before buying any equipment at all you should find out what things will be the most versatile. What tents and sleeping bags, for instance, could be carried easily in a backpack or in bicycle panniers and could also be used on a family car camping trip? Which of the other items you are buying will be the lightest and, when folded or rolled, the least bulky? In other words, could you use them for backpacking as well as for family-car camping?

Obviously the more camping experience you have and the more you observe other people's camping equipment and methods, discussing problems with your fellow campers, the better prepared you'll be to make the right decision before plunking down your hard-earned cash. On the following pages in this section we've tried to assemble helpful facts that will get you started when you're ready to buy or merely sort out what you already have at home.

When you do buy, instead of loading yourself down with a lot of fad items, buy a few good-quality things that will last for many years. And shop around for them. Don't just buy what the first store has to offer. Look at what the expensive stores and those catering to mountain climbers have to offer as well as the discount stores and stores that sell scouting equipment. You'll learn that way. Once you become familiar with the various brands and styles and know what you need and want, you'll be able to take advantage of end-of-season sales and not wind up with some useless items that nobody else wanted just because you got them at a good discount.

Look at army surplus stores, too, but not until you have seen enough equipment in other stores and/or in use at campgrounds to recognize the differences in weights and materials of items you find there, such as jackets, sleeping bags and ponchos. For backpacking, army surplus items are sometimes too heavy, but they may be just the thing for car camping—good quality and at a reasonable price.

Good camping equipment may last you for many years—but only if you take care of it. When storing it, you should first be sure it is clean and completely dry and that you are putting it where it will stay that way. Don't fold plastics or coated fabrics so that there is a tight crease which can cause a leak. If you have room, roll them loosely. Separate tent stays or other metal parts designed to fit together and pack the pieces separately from the tent.

When you buy equipment of any kind, read the label and follow carefully any instructions given.


## General Information about Clothes, Sleeping Gear, Tarps and Tents


The primary function of clothes, sleeping gear, tarps and tents is to protect the body and keep it warm (or cool) and comfortable. Keep that in mind when looking at all the exciting displays of colorful camping gear in catalogues and store windows, and it will be a little easier for you to keep your head and sense of perspective. When you go shopping, here are some points pertinent to these items you should keep in mind:

• Many camping outfitters rent camping gear (even such things as sleeping bags) and sometimes will apply rental price against the purchase price if you decide to buy. We should point out, however, that a sizable deposit is required, and during busy seasons it may be necessary to make reservations well ahead of time.

• If you're handy with a needle, you may want to check into the do-it-yourself kits put out by some outfitters.

• Camping gear comes in beautiful bright colors and patterns, but before letting the clerk wrap your selections, ask yourself these questions:

Will it look dirty after the first day's camping?

Will I get tired of this color (maybe you've fallen under the spell of a Chinese red or international orange tent) after a year or two?

Will I be able to combine (if it's an article of clothing) and color-coordinate it with my everyday clothes to get maximum use from it?

Before buying a snow- or sand-colored parka (or tent), ask yourself: Will I someday be camping where my life might depend on my companions' or a plane's spotting this parka (or tent) from a long distance away?

• Zippers whether on clothes or equipment should be sewn in so they don't catch on seam edges (try them), and they should be rust- and freeze-proof (such as nylon). If

they do stick, lubricate them with a little soap or candle wax
—never with oil.

• Double-stitched seams are stronger than those held together with a single line of stitching. Seams in which edges of
fabric have been folded under and interlocked, then double-
stitched, are most durable of all. Chain stitch (the underside
resembles a chain) is not so good as a lock-type stitch because, if the chain-stitched thread breaks, the whole line of
stitching can very quickly come unraveled.

• Camping clothes, sleeping bags and tents should be
made of closely woven, smooth material that will not snag
easily. The higher the thread count (number of threads
woven into a given area of cloth), the tougher and more
water-repellent but also the heavier the material will be.
Nylons in which you can see a fine line of reinforcing thread
are less apt to rip than ordinary nylon fabric and are called
"rip stop."

*The material should also be able to breathe.* For this reason, fabrics should not be plastic or coated with waterproof
substances. Exceptions to this rule are tarps, flies that extend
over tent tops, tent floors and ground cloths for tents and sleeping bags, and rain clothes such as ponchos worn only for rain;
these should be waterproof, not merely water-repellent.

• When purchasing an item, find out how it should be
cared for. Can your down parka or sleeping bag be machine-
washed (warm or cold water?) and machine-dried, or must it
go to a dry cleaner? *If you do take it to a dry cleaner, it must
be one who is experienced in handling down, and you should
air your sleeping bag to get rid of the fumes before using it.*
Can you buy a mending kit for the tent, tarp or mattress you
purchased? Is it all right to use a needle to sew up tears or
put on patches or must they be repaired with an adhesive?

• The characteristics of insulation are covered in the
"Sleeping Bags" section.

## Clothes

The clothes you will need to take with you will be deter-
mined by weather, where you are going and what you expect
to be doing. For at least the first few overnight or weekend

trips you should be able to get by with the clothes you have, so we give you the following rundown just as a rough guide and not as a mandate.

Take as few clothes as possible, just enough to keep you warm and reasonably clean—and, of course, to provide for any emergencies that may occur, especially to children. You should have extra socks both for hiking and because your feet may get dirtier and sweatier in camp than at home; otherwise about the same number of changes of under and outer clothes as you wear at home should be adequate.

You should have a hat or cap with a visor to shield the eyes and a crown that will provide some dead-air space insulation and maybe sunglasses. If your hair or a collar won't shield the back of your neck, consider a brimmed hat (one that stays on easily or can be tied on). Inez always carries a lightweight scarf to wear when she doesn't need a hat but wants to control her hair or add a little warmth.

The casual attitude toward the way we dress that has evolved in the past few years makes it wonderfully easy to prepare for sightseeing or other activities almost anywhere without taking along clothes that can't double for camping. But a woman sometimes likes her hair to look nice and there's nothing like a high-crowned, brimmed hat to help her cover up pin curls and still look the way she likes to look until she's ready to comb out her hair.

A brimmed hat is also convenient for tying a piece of mosquito netting around (beekeeper fashion), when hiking through country infested with troublesome bugs. At home cut the pieces of netting to the right size and figure out how to fasten them in place before starting on your trip. One way is simply to cut a circle and sew a piece of elastic around the outer edge. You may be able to buy suitably cut and finished pieces of netting.

The clothes you wear on the way to camp, with the possible exception of shoes, should be the ones you will also wear in camp for the rest of the day, thus cutting down on the number of changes you need to take and on the time wasted in changing.

Colors that don't show the dirt are best. If you'll be hiking during hunting season, wear a bright red or orange hat or jacket so any trigger-happy hunter can tell at a glance you are not his prey. If possible, find out where hunters are likely to be and stay far away from there.

Fabrics that don't wrinkle and are of a firm, close weave that won't tear easily or catch on shrubbery yet will absorb perspiration are best under most circumstances. However, at most improved campgrounds you can generally get by with the things you wear around the yard at home. Because of the stooping and bending connected with camp activity, you may want to wear looser-fitting garments for greater freedom.

Short pants and short sleeves may keep you cool in hot weather, but they have drawbacks. Your arms and legs can get painfully sunburned or scratched by branches (if you're in the woods), and you'll get more bug bites than if you are covered up. If you don't want to take extra clothes to fit the situation whatever it may be, the best answer is lightweight long sleeves and pants, but loose-fitting enough to be rolled up if you like.

If you're riding a bicycle, be sure your pants legs won't get caught in the gears. Some bikes have covered gear; if yours doesn't, a bicycle clip to control your pants legs may be in order.

At the end of Part I we cautioned beginners to camp only when and where they know the weather and travel conditions will be moderate. However, when venturing forth to spend a night or two in Mother Nature's province, you never know for sure just how low she may capriciously decide to turn her thermostat. This is especially true in high country, where it can be very warm during the day, but the temperature will suddenly drop to a chilling low at sundown and sometimes stay that way until well after the sun comes up in the morning. What to do? Be prepared. This doesn't mean that you need to start right out buying expensive down vests, jackets or parkas. (They are marvelously lightweight and warm and pack away into almost nothing and therefore are great for backpacking.) Not at least until you've become an experienced hiker and have started going out in the snowy season or you are heading upward ever higher into the cold, clear atmosphere of the beautiful, beckoning mountaintops.

The simplest thing is to take along a warm sweater or

thick woolen shirt and a roomy, tightly woven windbreaker, jacket or coat to wear over it. Still not enough? Insulated underwear should take care of just about any situation. (Don't buy the cheapest kind or they won't add much warmth.) Top it all off with a woolen cap you can pull down over your ears, a woolen scarf and warm gloves.

As we said, these are just suggestions. You can make up any combination of suitable garments you happen to have. A pair of tights, for instance, can add a lot of warmth under a pair of jeans just as well as under a skirt.

Speaking of tights reminds us that maybe you're a person with a bit of flesh on your thighs (one, let us say, who enjoys the good culinary life) right where they rub together uncomfortably when you walk, causing chafing, and maybe this makes you decide against taking those interesting hikes at camp. May even make you hesitate about going camping. Well, there's a very simple solution. Wear long, snug-fitting *cotton* underpants, the kind that extend at least halfway to the knee. Even in the summertime you'll find them wonderfully comfortable, and the problem of chafing will disappear.

Shoes should be given very careful consideration because almost all camping that's any fun requires that you use your feet somewhat more often and on rougher terrain than you do at home.

In the car and around a camp that's not rough or rocky (as is the case in many improved campgrounds), you can wear sneakers, loafers, comfortable oxfords or moccasins, in other words, low-heeled everyday knockabout shoes—so long as they are well broken-in and comfortable.

For hikes on rough or rocky trails, you should have a good, well-fitted and well-broken-in, comfortable laced-up pair of leather boots that are not heavy. They should have good-gripping rubber or composition soles, and the boot tops should cover your ankles but not extend much higher than that unless you're in snake country. Most people find a good-quality thick but soft wool sock the most comfortable foot covering for inside the boot. Some, for more rugged hiking than beginning campers usually do, wear two pairs. Have a good shoeman fit your boot over the wool socks, so you'll have plenty of toe room. If you find woolen socks uncomfortable, he may recommend heavy-pile Orlon or some combination of materials that will absorb the perspiration and keep your feet dry. Nylon, unless mixed with wool or Orlon, will overheat your feet.

Unless you are going on really rough trails, don't let it worry you if your children insist on wearing sneakers. But, if possible, see to it that they are good-quality over-the-ankle gym shoes.

Ask your shoeman's advice about what to put on the boots as a protection against moisture, but don't use anything that will close the pores and make them completely waterproof, as they need to breathe so your feet won't become soaking wet from perspiration.

Don't forget to take large-size Band-Aids along on your hikes to protect any spots that get rubbed by your shoe or boot. Apply one *before* the spot becomes a blister. "Moleskin" or "molefoam" (buy it at your drug or sporting-goods store) is even better than Band-Aids.

Keep your toenails cut short if you want to enjoy your walk.

If it's a long hike, stop at least once along the way and wash your feet with a cupful of water from your canteen (you should be carrying one on a long hike unless you know there is water along the way). You can stick a clean washcloth in your pocket to dry your feet. Carry a plastic sandwich bag along to put the washcloth in when it's damp from use.

Don't let the stop lull you into resting for more than a few minutes or your muscles will stiffen and thus will spoil your fun.

Find your walking rhythm, keep going and stick with the rhythm, even when moving slowly.

For boating you'd better take along a pair of sure-grip boat sneakers to help you navigate over slick decks or other surfaces. Never wear leather or any other smooth soles in a boat.

Besides your regular shoes and boots for any rough hiking, you'll probably want a pair of all-purpose beach-type sandals to wear around a pool and also in a public shower room.

Pockets come in very handy for stowing small, lightweight items. Patch pockets should be double-stitched or they may pull loose from a garment if you give them much use. You can usually add the second row of stitching very easily yourself.

That seems to cover just about all the clothes you'd need for a beginners' overnight or weekend camping trip, except for swim, rain and sleep gear.

All we'll say about swim suits is not to forget to take them along. Even if your campground doesn't provide a pool, river, lake or ocean, you may pass a place where you'd like to take a dip on your way to or from. So pack swim suits, towels, robes and beach shoes in two separate duffel bags (one for boys' dressing room, one for girls') and keep them readily available.

Since you're planning only an overnight or weekend trip, you may not want to bother with rain equipment but rather turn around and go home if the weather lets you down—or maybe stay overnight at a motel. Sometimes, off the beaten track, you may stumble onto a picturesque little old hotel that's reasonable and more fun than a motel. You can sit in the lobby after dinner (which you may be able to eat picnic style in your room if you have the right assortment of food in your cooler) and talk with the residents. Dan once met an old retiree in this way who had taken up gold panning as his way of finishing his journey through life. It was at Idaho Springs, Colorado, and we stayed over an extra day so Dan could go out with the happy old gent and try his own luck in a stream called Clear Creek that ran through the town. He didn't strike it rich, but then he didn't really expect to.

We think it gives a rewarding sense of accomplishment and well-being to stick it out, come rain or whatever (that's sort of what camping is all about), so we suggest, if you're buying rain gear for camping, buy ponchos—and be sure they extend at least to just below the knee. That way they'll deflect much of the rain away from your pant legs. Ponchos are more comfortable and they let more air circulate around your body than do raincoats, so you don't become overheated and wet from perspiration. They can also serve as ground covers or as makeshift tents. And if you go in for backpacking someday, you can wear a full-cut poncho over your pack (some are especially made for this purpose). Although most army equipment is scorned by backpackers as being too heavy, our son thinks the army poncho is very versatile and definitely worth considering. If you expect to be walking in heavy, windy downpours, you may also want to invest in waterproof chaps to slip on over your pants. But if the weather is warm, you're better off rolling your pants up to keep them dry.

Whatever your rain gear, keep it handy so you don't have to unpack a lot of other gear to get to it.

It's a good idea to have a good pair of old-fashioned heavy-duty rubbers to fit over your boots (or rubber boots to wear over sneakers and such) in case you go walking when it's wet. Hiking in a light drizzle or immediately after a rainstorm can be a thrilling experience for those sensitive people who have an eye for beauty. Leaves are washed and wet, and, when the sun comes out, sparkling diamonds are liberally sprinkled about in a way that would put a Tiffany window display to shame. Soils turn a richer, darker brown and nature's more subtle fragrances are released.

Unless you travel in a fully equipped recvee, you'll be using the campground's bathhouse and toilet facilities and will probably feel both comfortable sleeping and at ease walking around the camp in plain cotton pajamas. Substitute cuddly warm winter weights or insulated underwear if the weather is cold. If it's very cold, you may even want to don that woolen cap we mentioned earlier and maybe one of those extra pairs of socks, too.

As far as personal grooming supplies go, well, that's pretty much up to you and what you're used to. Bring as few as possible, maybe two sets, one for those going to the ladies' washroom and one for the men's. In addition, you should have a good first-aid kit.

Your first-aid kit should contain any prescription medication you require plus such things as: adhesive tape, moleskin or molefoam, assorted sizes of Band-Aids, a roll of gauze bandage, absorbent cotton, antiseptic, burn ointment, calamine lotion, Chapstick, snakebite kit, sunburn lotion, scissors and tweezers. It's a good idea to keep with the kit a small first-aid booklet, one that includes instructions for mouth-to-mouth resuscitation, that you'd already read before leaving home. And, as a little added insurance, carry along a cake of yellow soap and, if anyone thinks he has touched poison ivy or poison oak, he should wash his hands and the area of contact thoroughly with it as soon after contact as possible.

A terry cloth swimming robe, or a coat or windbreaker can make do as a bathrobe to wear over pajamas. And unless the campground happens to be paved, you'll probably want to wear your regular shoes in getting to and from the bathhouse; otherwise, your beach shoes can double as bed slippers.

If for additional warmth you plan on wearing to bed the underclothes that you've worn all day, don't. Even though they don't feel damp, they'll have absorbed moisture from your body during the day.

Don't lay out clean underclothes and socks for the next morning's wear. Leave them in the duffel bag, where they won't get drenched with dew. And remember also to leave outer garments you are going to wear a second day where they won't become dew-drenched, perhaps in the car with the windows rolled up (if no one is sleeping there), perhaps folded up beneath a tarp. A little camping experience will sharpen your ingenuity until you're outwitting nature's mischievous little ways at every turn. And that will make you so confident that you'll soon be passing your ideas on to fellow campers. One of the things about camping that's good for us is that manufacturers can't quite do *all* of our work and thinking for us, and for a brief time we can shed that disturbing feeling of being one of science's robots.

## Blankets, Mattresses, Sleeping Bags, Cots, etc.

If you're going overnight or weekend camping in your car (or by boat) in mild weather where the temperature can be depended on not to drop very low at night, you can be very comfortable sleeping beneath the blankets right off your bed. But not quite the way the TV and movie cowboys do it—not on the bare ground with one thin blanket wrapped around you. Without much trouble at all, you can do better than that.

If you're going to be sleeping on the ground, find a spot that's smooth and as level as possible; if not level, place your head uphill for greatest comfort. Brush away any sticks and pebbles. Lay out a tarpaulin or a waterproof ground cloth. This can be one you bought at a sporting goods or camping store or it can be a sheet of plastic you had around the house, maybe an old tablecloth or shower curtain. It may even be a "space" blanket, an item made of polyethylene, aluminum and fiberglass which makes use of a principle developed for the astronauts and, when the aluminum side is turned toward a person, stops virtually all radiation heat loss. It's a very lightweight (and easily folded into pocket-carrying size), handy item to have around camp.

Next, if you want to both be comfortable and insulate yourself from the cold, spread out one of two kinds of mattresses:

**1. Foam:** This can be foam mattresses or pillows borrowed from beds and chairs at home. Our nephew, the one we mentioned earlier who now camps in a cottage tent with seven children, originally went station-wagon camping when the kids numbered only five. He took along the foam mattresses from two rather wide bunk beds, putting one of them in the back of the station wagon for four children (the littlest slept in a car bed on the front seat). He and his wife made up their bed with the other mattress on the grass at the side of the station wagon.

We have heard of other campers who built a ¾-inch-thick plywood platform in the back of their station wagon. They put legs under all four corners and at least one very sturdy leg in the center. The platform was about one foot high, and they slid boxes and bags of supplies underneath it and put a foam-rubber mattress on top of it. That way, they could leave their bed made up when they traveled and didn't have to move all their supplies in order to use it. Of course, this arrangement is only good for two people, unless a third one is very small and can ride in the front seat in the middle and sleep in the back without crowding things too much. The success of this arrangement depends as much on temperament as on dimensions.

We have a set of chairs with removable foam cushions (seat, back and footstool). Each set, fitted together, makes a very comfortable mattress for one person; the two sets, if pushed together side by side, make a fair-sized double bed.

You can also buy foam pads or mattresses. The closed-cell type of foam stays dry and permits no movement of air; however, it is not so comfortable as open-cell foam. If you might someday use the pad for backpacking, you will want to buy a very lightweight thin one specifically designed for that purpose.

**2. Air Mattress:** The cheaper variety of air mattress is made of plastic and is subject to easy puncture. It's also likely to be so slippery you'll have difficulty not sliding off. The better kind is made of rubberized cloth, and although it too can be punctured, it doesn't happen so easily, especially with the better-made ones. One that is moderately priced should give you good service.

Air mattresses must be blown up, of course, and for this you will need an air pump. The pump should be separate from the mattress itself, and *not* one that is built into the mattress, because, if a built-in pump breaks, your mattress can no longer serve you. You should not use a service-station pump on your mattress. And one more very important *don't:* Don't be guided by the uninflated size when making your purchase or you may find yourself falling off the edge. One way to keep from falling off the edge of an air mattress is not to fill it too full of air. It will be very comfortable if your hips can sink to within a half-inch of the bottom. How do you mend those punctures we mentioned? Be sure instructions come with your mattress and buy whatever materials you will need *and take them with you.*

Both foam and air mattresses come in sizes specifically designed to fit into the back of your station wagon. If buying them for a tent, be sure they will fit inside!

In an emergency, if you don't have either a foam pad or an air mattress, but you do happen to save old newspapers, a good way to make use of them is to lay as many sheets as possible (the more sheets, the better the insulation), overlapping, between the ground cloth and the blanket roll or sleeping bag. They won't make the ground feel any softer, but they'll make you warmer, so maybe you'll sleep and not know the difference. Just be sure you pick them all up. The best way to dispose of them is to take them home with you. Burning a lot of paper in a campfire can be unsafe, because the flaming bits blow around. If you put them in a trash can, they may escape and blow around, making an unsightly mess.

Many backpackers who use mattresses prefer air to foam because it compresses (when unfilled) into a much more compact package, even though it may be heavier. Some buy a short-length mattress that will extend just below their knees.

As with most equipment, a little care will lengthen the life of your air mattress. Specifically, do not leave it in the sun; stand it up while inflated in a shady, airy place to dry. Do not clean it with such solvents as gasoline. When not in use, store away from heat, slightly inflated.

*If you're wondering why we don't romanticize the joys of a green bough mattress, we'll tell you. The trees in our forests can no longer spare their green boughs to provide mattresses for campers. In fact, you'll find no references in this book to cutting green wood for any use whatsoever. It's far more important that we conserve our trees and make do with something else.*

Now you're ready to make up a double (or triple, if the occupants are small) bed just as you would at home with sheets, pillows, the works—either on the ground, in the back of your station wagon, in a tent, or for little shavers, on the car seat. If you don't want to carry pillows along, at least bring the cases and fill them with clothes, towels or what have you. Use colored sheets and pillow cases if you have them, the darker, the better.

Thick, fluffy woolen blankets will keep you warmer than the tightly woven army type because they're thicker and their fuzziness catches and holds pockets of air, providing insulation, particularly if you cover the blankets with a closely woven, wind-repellent (*not* waterproofed) cover of some sort.

You can make your bed warmer by folding the edges of the two sides and the bottom of both sheets and all your blankets under and pin them with a dozen or so four-inch blanket safety pins.

Or, before you ever leave home, you can make up your own blanket (single person) sleeping bag. To do this, lay half of one blanket over half of another, and fold the two remaining single halves, one over the other. Then fold the bottom under and either pin it with blanket safety pins or sew it by hand with a large running stitch, using linen thread and a very heavy needle. Either pin or stitch the blanket bag about halfway up both sides. If you like, lay a sheet over the two half blankets that will go immediately under and over you before folding. Flannel sheets, by the way, if you happen to have such an old-fashioned item, will feel much warmer than the regular kind, but you won't slip into them so easily. You can add to the sleeping bag's warmth by starting with a sheet of closely woven, wind-repellent material and arrange the other two blankets and sheet on top of it. When all the folding is done, the wind-repellent sheet of cloth should form the bottom and top coverings of your bag. This should keep you warm in temperatures from 65° to 70° F. (if the wind doesn't blow too hard) and at considerably lower temperatures if you have an extra blanket to throw over you if need be and/or sleep in a tent or other shelter.

We mentioned this before under "Clothing," but it's worth reminding you: A cap that pulls down over your ears and a pair of socks (especially woolen ones) on your feet will raise your temperature considerably. A warm jacket to cover up the area that always seems to get uncovered, around the neck and shoulders, can help too. Or, if you have such a thing, a sleeveless turtleneck sweater.

Use your own ingenuity and you may come up with some methods of using your home bedding, especially for half-size sleeping bags, that are far better for you than the ones we have described. You may discover that your small children don't need mattresses. An old folded quilt may serve or extra layers of blankets in their homemade sleeping bags may do the trick. (Inez has fond memories of sleeping as a child on thick pads of dry pine needles at the side of mountain roads enroute to the family's Sierra Nevada summer campsite.) Just remember, if they don't sleep on mattresses, they will need something to replace the insulation the mattresses give and protect them from ground that's cold and/or damp —even inside a tent. If they sleep on the car seats, it will be much easier to keep them covered if they are in a sleeping bag.

**Sleeping Bags:** There's no doubt that sleeping bags are nice to have, but there are so many styles with new ones being constantly developed that it's very difficult to know which one to buy when you decide the time has come to invest in one or more.

The purpose of a sleeping bag is to insulate you from the cold, and it will perhaps help to know which bags are good and which are not (as well as which are most suitable for carrying on your back), if you consider them from a technical standpoint.

Most of us are familiar with the way insulation keeps our houses warm. We build a wall around us that keeps the cold air out and the warm air in. We put a roof on our house with dead-air space between it and the ceiling. We build double walls around the outside of our houses, with a layer of air between them. To improve the insulation provided by our walls and ceilings, we add a tremendous number of tiny pockets and layers of dead air by placing a mass of fiber between the walls and between the roof and the ceiling. The thicker the insulation, the warmer the house is.

The nearer our camping sleep gear comes to doing the

same thing, the warmer we will be. The outer cover of a sleeping bag should be made of a firm, tightly woven, wind- and water-resistant (not water*proof*, because it must breathe) fabric. The insulation which fills the space between the outer shell and the lining of a good bag is usually 100 percent fiberfill (Dacron is very good), goose or duck down, or perhaps even foam. Never buy a bag filled with wool, cotton or kapok or any reused substance. The thicker the layer of filler ("loft"), all other things being equal (workmanship, wind velocity, etc.), the warmer the sleeping bag will be.

Down from geese or ducks has been considered the best fill for sleeping bags because it is very light (it takes about twice the weight of some fiberfills to give comparable warmth) and because it compresses into a very small area yet fluffs back up again to its previous loft, with each little bit of fluff staying separate from the others.

It has one very big drawback: It's the most expensive of the sleeping-bag fillers. It also squashes down beneath the sleeper's body, making it necessary to use an air mattress or foam pad, both for comfort and to replace the lost insulation made by lowering the loft in that particular area.

The Coleman Company's regional manager, Bob Malay, tells us that a new fill is being marketed that has many of the properties of down with the good qualities of Dacron. It is called "Dacron II." He says it can be washed, it breathes but does not hold moisture given off by the body, it is nonallergenic, and does not tend to shift in the bag. Like down, it can be compacted into a small area and has similar warming qualities.

Our son uses a foam sleeping bag for backpacking and considers it a good, inexpensive substitute for down when the weather is not extremely cold. Although it's a little heavier and bulkier and not quite so warm, it doesn't squash flat beneath his body the way down does, so he doesn't need to carry a mattress.

The workmanship on a bag is, of course, of equal importance to the materials from which it is made. Quilting stitched all the way through from lining to outer cover may hold the insulating material in place but will leave cold spots along the stitching lines. The very best bags are so constructed as to avoid this. To advise you in such matters as this, when buying expensive bags, you should find a reputable outfitter. A prime A or double A Northern goosedown bag may sell for $80 on up, while you can get a good Dacron 88 bag for $25 and a good Dacron II bag beginning around $40, but they might not be equally suitable for your specific needs.

Zippers should be covered on the inside of the bag with a strip of weatherproofing material that protects you from both the possible roughness of the zipper itself and from cold spots.

Besides the variety of materials used in making sleeping bags, there are many different designs. The type you should have depends on what you will be doing.

Mummy bags look just like what their name implies and are designed for warmth and lightness. Therefore they are good cold-weather backpacking bags. They fit so closely to the body that there is little room for areas of cold air. They should have a hood that is either attached or snaps on and draws up closely around the face, so there is little space for warm air to escape at the neck. However, some people find them too confining and therefore uncomfortable.

The opposite extreme to a mummy bag is a rectangle, which is very roomy. While it is very comfortable, there is a lot of room for cold air that the body must heat, and it is less conservative of material and therefore heavier than the mummy.

A large, slim mummy bag may be filled with enough down to give a six-and-a-half-inch loft, yet weigh no more than three pounds and will keep you warm at 10° F. A semirectangular bag weighing four pounds may keep you warm at 20° F., all other factors being equal. Try to find out when buying a sleeping bag at what temperature you can expect to stay warm in it. A good salesman should be able to give you a pretty good idea. But you must remember this: Different people need different amounts of insulation to feel comfortable, and the same person can react differently at different times, depending on such things as how well he has eaten that day and how fatigued he is. Wind is also a big factor in reducing the warmth of the sleeping bag. So the ability of any bag to keep you warm will depend in part on the degree to which you are protected from the wind and other weather factors such as degree of moisture in the air.

There are all variations of shape in between the slimmest mummy and the full rectangle. Many bags that open down one side and completely across the bottom can be zipped together into a double bag. Two people sleeping together conserve more heat than one person sleeping alone. These bags have other advantages. They can be completely opened out, fluffed up, and hung out to air (which should be done every day a bag is used, if possible), and they serve as extra quilts on cold winter nights at home. (We have found that sleeping bags seldom go to waste even when not being used for camping, because besides serving as quilts they also serve as extra beds when we have lots of company. Children think it a great lark when a whole crowd of them spread out on the floor in sleeping bags.)

Another feature of sleeping bag design is known as the differential cut, meaning that the outer covering is cut larger than the inner lining to maintain the loft. Differential seems to work better in slim mummy bags than in the others. In roomier bags the lining tends to pull away from the body and leave cold-air space.

Speaking of lining, we highly recommend that you buy and use washable liners with your bag. You won't have to wash or have it cleaned so often and it will serve you longer.

Most good bags will have a pocket into which you can slide a mattress—and which also serves to protect the bag's quilt stitching from snags—but you may not find the arrangement comfortable and prefer to leave the mattress and sleeping bag separate. However, if you are going to use the pocket, you will have to buy a mattress designed to fit into it.

Some bags have a waterproof rainshield that extends over the sleeper's head. Since a sleeping bag itself should not be waterproof, a rainshield covering just your head doesn't do you much good unless you can use it in conjunction with a waterproof tarp or poncho. Or you may find it useful as a frame to support mosquito netting.

You'll want a waterproof stuff-bag to pack your sleeping bag in. It's a good idea to buy them together so you can be sure the two items are the right size for each other.

Be sure sleeping bags are completely dry before storing them. Don't squash them down any more than necessary when storing, and be sure to follow any specific instructions that come with your bag.

When our great-niece Rebecca Kraemer went tent camping with her parents at the age of five months, she was very content dressed in a bunting that had sleeves and a hood. She slept in the familiar bed part of her baby carriage which had been simply lifted out of its frame.

If you take a baby camping, be sure the underside of the bed he sleeps in is well insulated. Any air moving beneath the bed will have a chilling effect.

**Cots and Hammocks:** If you sleep in a cot or a hammock, you'll feel the chilling effect of any air that moves beneath you. One way you can diminish the chill is to put a space blanket underneath you with the radiating side turned toward your body.

For an overnight or weekend trip you may prefer not to bother with cots and sleep just with a mattress placed on a ground cloth so you automatically eliminate the problem of underside chill from moving air. But for those of you who get a sense of security from being above the ground or if you're sleeping in snake country, there are many styles of cots and several different styles of hammocks.

Among others, there's a very lightweight nylon net hammock, and there's a jungle hammock complete with mosquito netting and a waterproof fly that is sometimes available at army surplus stores. Most people don't find hammocks very comfortable for sleeping. If you're different from most people and decide you want to take a hammock along when you go camping, don't forget that you'll need to find trees to hang it from.

Various cots that fold up into compact sizes and/or come apart into various pieces are available. Here's a rundown of some of the things to keep in mind when buying:

• Will you get maximum use from it? For instance, can one end be raised so you can use the cot as a lounge chair at camp or in the yard at home? Is it comfortable enough to use at home sometimes as a spare bed for guests?

• Will all the cots you plan on buying fit in your tent (if you plan on using a tent)? Remember when measuring that most tents taper inward from bottom to top, so make allowances.

• If the cot has parts that come apart, can you assemble and disassemble it with ease? Try it well ahead of time so that, if it doesn't work as advertised, you can return it and make other arrangements. Also check to see if some parts may be missing!

• Are the legs constructed so they won't poke holes in the ground cloth or tent floor?

• Remember, if the bed is not constructed to be comfortable or if the weather turns chilly, you will want a mattress or padding of some kind that will fit on it.

**Mosquito Netting and Insecticides:** To varying degrees campground managers spray their grounds with insecticides, and there are quite effective "foggers" available. But regulations concerning the use of insecticides are constantly changing, and people are becoming a bit more cautious about smearing just any old repellent on their skin. Tentmakers tell us that insecticides should not be sprayed on tent fabrics, as the effectiveness of the water repellents may be destroyed.

So, all in all, mosquito netting still remains one of the greatest contributions man has made to comfortable camp sleeping. The most important job is to secure all the openings in your tent against any possible attempted invasions, that is, if you are sleeping in a tent. If you are not and if there are biting bugs around, then you may find the netting covers made to go over individual cots or sleeping bags just the thing to give you a good night's rest and thwart the invaders. And don't forget to bring netting covers for baby's bed, too. If you are going to be sleeping in your station wagon, screens are available in sizes that will fit the windows. You can buy netting by the yard if you can't get the protection you want and prefer to make it yourself. And you can buy self-sticking plastic screen patches in case your netting gets holes in it. Whether you buy something already made up or not, be sure the netting is fine enough to keep all bugs out. At this writing, nylon mesh seems to be the best.

And before buying any repellents, either "foggers" or the

kind you apply to your skin, find out if they are the most recently developed. Don't buy stuff that's been sitting on the shelf for several years. It may contain something that's been found to be harmful either to nature or to you—after all, you're part of nature, aren't you?

## Tarps and Tarp Shelters

Although a tarp (tarpaulin) was originally a sheet of canvas made more waterproof by treating it with tar, the term now is used to describe almost any flat sheet of waterproof or water-repellent material, sometimes canvas, sometimes plastic. Old shower curtains, tablecloths, etc. can be very useful, and if waterproofing isn't necessary, you can use a closely woven bedspread or some such thing. If weight is a factor as in backpacking, then lightweight plastic or coated nylon is very good. If you buy a sheet of material specifically intended as a tarpaulin, it may have grommets or tabs on all four sides so that you can either peg it or tie it down or hang it up in a number of ways for any number of uses. Either the grommets should be on the doubled-over hem of the tarp material, or the area where they or the tabs are fastened should be reinforced in some other way, so they won't pull out easily, leaving a weak spot that, especially in plastic, will soon tear. If the tarp doesn't have grommets or tabs, you can lay a small, smooth stone where they would normally be, gather the material around the stone and tie around it with one end of a piece of light cord. Then you can tie the other end of the cord to a stake or whatever you might want to fasten it to. Or buy some gadgets called "Visklamps," which are expressly made for this purpose. Or, if your tarp isn't too heavy and the wind isn't blowing very hard, you can simply use spring-type clothespins as fasteners for some purposes and forget about tying. (Thank you, Priscilla Strung, for the clothespin method.)

With a little ingenuity, the ways and means of using a tarp around camp are almost endless. Here are a few:

• Use it enroute to cover the things you've packed on the roof of your car.

• Lay it on the ground and unload on it items you want to protect from moist earth or dirt.

• Spread it over duffel bags and other gear in a rainstorm, securing it around the bottom with rocks or other weights.

• Spread it over a camp cooler to provide extra insulation.

• In the woods you can suspend it (by attaching lines to the corners) from four trees as a fly, giving protection from the sun and/or the rain. It can even be used in this way or tied in some other manner as a shield over your tent, making your accommodations more waterproof in a rainstorm and adding a dimension of insulation. Or it can be used this way to shield the cooking and eating area or children's play area from sun and/or rain.

• You can wrap it around trees or suspend it from branches with clothespins to make a dressing room or give privacy to a portable toilet.

• If it's waterproof, you can use it as a ground cloth for sleeping bags or tent.

And, if that is not enough, one of the best uses of all for a tarp is as a sleeping shelter if you are not carrying a tent or if everybody doesn't fit into the tent.

*There are some campgrounds that insist that campers sleep within a shelter of some kind. If you always have a tarp and the necessary line, etc. to turn it into a tent, you will be able to comply with any such regulations.*

**The Tarp as a Lean-To Shelter:** String a length of clothesline through the grommets or tabs on one side of a tarp. If the tarp slides toward the center of the line, stuff twigs or bits of cloth into the grommet or tab holes. If the tarp doesn't have such refinements, fold the edge over the clothesline and fasten securely with plenty of good-quality, spring-type clothespins. Peg down the corners of the opposite side of the tarp either by driving stakes through the grommets or tabs or by driving the stakes into the ground and running cords from them to the grommets or tabs. Then tie the two ends of the line to two trees and finish pegging down the ground side. If there are no grommets or tabs to drive stakes through or tie them to, tie them with short pieces of cord to the pebble assemblies we described earlier.

Bring along wooden stakes at least a foot long, or, much

better, buy good-quality metal tent stakes from a camping-goods store. If you are backpacking and don't want to carry stakes, you may be able to whittle them at camp or improvise in some way such as tying your tarp to a log.

The variations of the way you can make a lean-to are many. If you aren't camping in the woods, you can, for instance, run a line all the way around the top of your car and tie both ends to the tarp. Then peg down the low side (or end, depending on which way you arrange it) of the tarp.

If you have an extra long tarp, you might be able to figure out ways of letting one end drop down and fastening it, thereby at least partially closing in that end of the shelter.

You can use the rock assembly to fasten a couple of cords to seams half or three-quarters of the way down from the top of your lean-to, then tie the loose ends to trees or something else to keep the top of your shelter from sagging down over you.

You can throw the tarp over a canoe laid on its side—or over a picnic table—and peg down both ends. The length of any pegging lines will depend on the dimensions of the tarp. Just be sure you bring along plenty of pegs and line for any situation that develops. Be sure the line you bring to tie through grommets and around stakes is strong enough to hold, but at the same time light enough to manipulate easily. If you are backpacking, weight may be a factor too.

*The Tarp as a Pup-Tent Shelter:* The tarp pup tent is made in almost the same way as the first example of a lean-to, using a line tied between two trees. But when erecting the pup tent, throw the tarp over the line with equal amounts of material on both sides of the line and peg down both ends of the tarp. A row of clothespins along the tent ridge will keep the material from bunching.

If you make use of some of that good old camper's ingenuity we keep mentioning, you can make all kinds of variations on those two basic themes. Just one example: You can fasten a small tarp with clothespins to one end of the pup tent to give more privacy.

You can hang (and peg down) two small tarp halves from both ends of a lean-to to foil either probing eyes or those probing fingers of wind that can't seem to make up their mind whether they're going to blow from the rear or the left or the right.

Closed in this way, and with a bonfire built against a hill or rock that reflects the fire's warmth into the open side of the lean-to, you can be as cozy as a bug in a rug. Just be careful and don't build a fire near to material that's not fire-retardant. *As a matter of fact, you should only use fire-retardant material for any fly or shelter.* And naturally put the fire out before going to sleep!

A little practice at home will make building a tarp shelter at camp a whole lot easier. If you don't have trees to string your line between, use your clothesline or your neighbor's if you don't have one. Experimenting with an old sheet before buying will give you a good idea of the size tarp you'll need for the use you intend putting it to.

You'll see pictures in books showing tarps combined with branches cut from trees to make lean-tos and tents. Don't do this. Our woods are too precious to misuse in such a way.

## Tents

If you decide that you want something for your weekend or overnight camping trip that gives you a bit more protection than the tarp shelters we've described, you can have almost any type, shape, size or color of tent you want. The choice available is so wide that to walk in and pick one out just like that can't be done. You have to find some way, or better yet, some *ways* to narrow your selection down.

The first step in that direction is easy. Since you're looking only for an overnight or weekend shelter, don't burden yourself with a large, heavy "cottage" or "bungalow" type that is designed for living in for from a week to two months, somewhat as you would use your house. What you need is a small tent that will give your family just enough shelter for sleeping comfortably for one or two nights, just big enough to give you shelter from the wind and the rain and offer dressing privacy if, perchance, you don't happen to be camping at a campground where there are adequate facilities available. So the height of the tent may be a factor. Do you feel you must stand up when dressing, or for one or two days and nights in a row can you manage to pull on your clothes in a sitting position?

One of the most popular tents which gives enough room to stand up is the "umbrella." It has an exterior aluminum frame that comes apart in sections and can be easily and quickly erected or taken down by one person. The sizes start around seven feet by seven (we don't recommend getting one quite this small), and, besides being a good tent for overnight or weekends, it's also good for a long trip on which you do your sleeping in the car or tent rather than at a motel.

Another tent that's popular among weekend campers is a small (ten feet by eight feet) cabin style that can be very quickly erected.

You can buy either a good small umbrella- or a cabin-style tent for $60 and up.

If you or your children may someday take up backpacking, you may want to get by with a lightweight backpacking tent for your first one. Some families start out with a backpacking tent; then, as the children get a little older and no longer fit on the car seats, and longer camping trips enter the picture, a larger (and heavier) cottage-style tent also is acquired. Small pop tents (tents that pop up somewhat on the same principle as an umbrella) may be suitable for children who want their own tent, but don't get one that's too cheap or it may not go up and down so easily as advertised.

You may be confused by all the tent shapes in a showroom and it will help a little if you stop to consider that there was a reason for making it in that particular form, at least when the particular shape was first designed.

Steeply sloping roofs and sides shed the rain, whereas a flat roof collects it in a pool from which it may eventually drip into the interior. But the steep sides also cut down on headroom inside the tent.

When the sun is shining brightly there doesn't seem to be any reason for adding considerable expense to have a waterproof floor extend a few inches up the sides of a tent. But the improvement it makes becomes obvious when the mud starts splashing on fabric and runoff from the rain soaks through the bottom of the sides of a tent that doesn't have that guard and are only water-repellent, not waterproof.

A tent wide open in the front and with a sloping rear was originally designed for campers who liked to sit in its shelter while the heat from a campfire came through the opening, bounced off the sloping rear and toasted the occupants as if they were biscuits in a reflector oven. But a more esthetic reason for the front end of a tent to be wide open is so that the occupants can get a more all-encompassing view of the stars at night and the pastels of a dawn sky than they do when sealed up in their houses and apartments at home. Of course, it's hard to make an efficient door to close the entire front of a tent. It's hard to bug-proof it, too. But then everything has its price.

A pop tent, which doesn't rely on stakes to hold it, was designed that way partly for ease of erection, but also so it could be used on sand, where stakes do not hold very well. But the shape is such that an adult would feel like a doughnut trying to sleep in a small one, and it wouldn't be wise to set one up near the edge of a cliff in high-wind country.

That is the way it is with most tent features; for every advantage, there's a disadvantage. So pick the features that are most important to you and accept the disadvantages as a true camper should, as a challenge—one that sends you home after a two-day outing feeling far more satisfied with yourself than when you left.

We have only mentioned a few of the more common names of tent designs. There are many more, but to try to describe them all here would only be confusing.

So, as we said, go to the store, look over the array of tents, study them, read the labels, then ask the clerk to explain any of the features you don't understand and to make recommendations. Then, if you are not completely satisfied that you are making a wise choice, try to rent the style you have chosen, and, if possible, apply the rent against any purchase you make.

Something you may want to hold in your minds for future planning (if you are a family) is the fact that some tents are designed to be zipped together in a variety of versatile ways.

But there are other considerations besides basic design which you should keep in mind when choosing a tent. Here are some of them:

Tents, as we mentioned briefly at the beginning of this chapter, must be able to breathe for the user to be comfortable and so that the moisture an occupant's body constantly gives off won't collect on the ceiling and drip back down on him. So tent materials (except for the floor, which may also extend a short distance up the tent side) cannot be waterproof.

Therefore, they are usually made of cotton (which expands when wet so that it almost entirely seals up the air space between threads, making the fabric quite water-repellent) or cotton and a synthetic (most often Dacron), the synthetic being added to lighten the weight of the cotton. Both materials may be referred to either as canvas, cotton, drill, duck or by any one of a number of trade names. To avoid confusion, we limit ourselves to the term "canvas."

When the rain first starts to wet the tent, a fine spray may come through the holes between the threads in the fabric, but these will soon seal.

There are also many nylon tents, but they are usually the small backpacking types. The reason nylon is used for them is that it is fairly strong, can be rolled up into a *very* compact parcel and is exceptionally lightweight and easy to carry. It is not used very often for the larger tents because it is not so breathable as canvas and does not hold up so well (it will fray) under the kind of all-day use a large tent is designed to take.

Nylon does not expand when wet as canvas does, so either the tent or a fly over it may be treated with a waterproofing material to keep it from leaking. If you buy a nylon tent, be sure it has a good-sized door and cross ventilation from at least one good-sized window. You will also have to treat the seams occasionally with a sealer or they may leak where needles have penetrated the fabric.

Prices for good-quality backpacking tents range from about $45 to $150.

Not all but most canvas tents are treated with some substance to make them more water-repellent. The cheaper tents may be treated with paraffin or some other oil product, and these finishes are very flammable and may add considerable weight while giving the impression that the fabric is stouter than it actually is. Others, generally the better tents, may be treated with a compound containing a fire-resistant chemical. It's generally the "dry" or "very dry" finishes that are most fire-retardant; these terms also usually indicate that a mildew-retardant has been used.

*One of the most important reasons for buying from a reliable camping outfitter is that you can ask him if your tent is as flame-retardant as possible and have confidence in his reply.* Regulations governing this aspect of tent fabrics (and sleeping-bag fabrics, too, we believe) are being considered in some states. While you're checking your tent, check the ropes that come with it (or extra ones you may buy) to see if they, too, are fire-retardant.

A really well-made canvas tent that is given the proper care and has been treated with one of the highest-quality water and mildew repellents will last you for many years, and the treatment will not wear off as it will in a cheaper tent. When the treatment does come off a tent, you can renew it with a brush or a spray, but follow the instructions and watch that you don't apply too much of the substance or the tent won't breathe.

You should be able to fasten tent windows and doors securely against a storm. Some zip shut, some are merely flaps that tie shut and may not give complete protection against wind-driven rain. Some windows can be fastened shut from the inside of the tent (most better tents are in this class) and some have to be fastened from outside. Some awnings also serve as doors, and when so used they obviously do not give much protection against a rainstorm while you remove boots and rain gear before entering the tent. The awning should be wide enough to mean something.

Mosquito netting should be very durable and of very fine mesh. The finer meshes, as we said previously, are usually nylon. Black flies will go through fiberglass mesh.

Almost all tents today have a sewn-in waterproof floor, and most of them have a strip of fabric several inches high at the base of the door to protect from things that crawl, snakes and such.

Some tents (most often, backpacking nylons) come equipped with a fly (sometimes waterproofed, sometimes not and sometimes attached and sometimes not) that goes over the top for additional protection from rain and for additional insulation. You can buy a separate fly if you want and rig it over any tent.

Stakes should be strong and they should be at least a foot long, longer if you are going to set up the tent in muddy or sandy soil (there are special types of stakes made for beach and desert sand). If the stakes with your tent aren't adequate, buy some that are. Nothing is more discouraging than a bent tent stake, so play it safe and take extras, preferably at least four that are about 18 inches long.

Telescoping poles are convenient, but, especially when they come with cheaper tents, they may get bent and be difficult to operate. Tents with the supports outside the tent are easier to erect than those with the old-style interior supports, but the design of the tent should determine which type your tent has, and the expert advice of a good outfitter is essential because of the constant design modifications that take place. Poles should be lightweight but very strong (aluminum is the best material), and those which break down into several sections should fit together and come apart without difficulty. Always take the pieces apart, dry thoroughly and store separately from the tent as soon as you take the tent down.

How big should the tent be? That, as Will Shakespeare would say, is the question! People come in all shapes and sizes, and the size of the people in your family, those who will be sleeping in the tent, determines the size of your tent. You can use the manufacturers' estimates (two-man tent, three-man tent, etc.) only as a rough guide. So, before you make your final decision, lie down together on the living-room carpet and measure how much space you need to be comfortable.

Keep these things in mind:

• Unless the sides of your tent are perpendicular, you will

have to allow for the slope in determining the height of the sleeper, mattress, cot, if any, and bedding.

*Canvas fabrics leak if touched when they are wet and they don't stop dripping until the rain stops and any collection of water on the exterior of the tent has evaporated, run off or run into the tent. So you'll have to establish the habit of never touching your tent when it's wet. Be prepared with a pan to put under the leak should you forget, and most important, buy a large enough tent so you can sleep comfortably without bumping against the walls.*

• If you touch wet nylon in a storm, it will feel damp but it won't drip.

• The minimum space usually allowed for a backpacking tent is about 18 usable square feet per person, which doesn't take into account shapes and sizes of the occupants. Another way of figuring for backpacker tents is roughly two and a half feet of width for each person multiplied by the length of the tallest sleeper. That figure will give you the absolute minimum of usable floor space you will need.

• Take this into account: You will need a bit of extra floor space (covered with newspapers or plastic) for wet boots unless you have some sort of weatherproof container you can leave them in just outside the door. You can usually hang most of your daytime clothes inside your car and lay the robe or coat you wear to the bathhouse dressing room on top of your bed. But if you're wearing a wet raincoat and there's no place to hang it in the tent, then you'll need a place you can loosely fold it and lay it on the floor (again, on newspapers or plastic). If you are using cots, the space underneath them can be utilized for storing the things we've mentioned. Sometimes the angle of space where the wall joins the floor will suffice. A lot depends on the design of the tent you choose, so keep all these things in mind when making your decision.

• When choosing among several tents, don't forget to compare the various weights, including supports. Find out why some are heavier than others. If one is heavier because the number of threads per square inch (thread count) is greater than in another tent, that is good, because the fabric will be stronger and more water-repellent. Of course, if weight is a factor, maybe it's not good after all. One tent may be heavier than another because cheap and inflammable paraffin "waterproofing" has been used on the fabric—and that's *not good*.

• And last, but not least, be sure the advertised size of the tent is the actual finished size and not the size of the pre-sewn material.

Take your tent home after you buy it, read all the instructions and check to see that you have all the parts. If something is missing, it's much better to find it out while you can still do something about it, not after you arrive at camp!

If you have a yard, set up your tent complete with waterproof ground cloth, just as if you were at camp. The ground cloth should not extend beyond the bottom of the tent or rain water will catch in it and run under the tent. If the tent is made of canvas, turn the sprinkler on it and give it a good soaking. If it gets excessively taut when wet, loosen the stays, stakes or whatever controls the tension so that there won't be too much stress on the fabric. (Some exterior supports are self-adapting.) If this proves to be necessary with your tent, remember to do the same thing at camp *before* you go to bed if you expect rain. Let your tent dry out and then make up the beds, complete with mattresses and cots (if any), and see how everything fits. Let the kids sleep there for a night or two, but the tent should not be considered a playhouse or an army fort if you want it to last. Turn the sprinkler on your tent a second time and note if the water drips enough at first that you should consider taking along a sheet of water-repellent cloth or plastic to cover the beds just during the first few minutes of a rainstorm. Sponge off any droppings or other soil with clear, cool water and let your tent dry thoroughly again (check the thick seams), hanging it over the line or draping it over yard furniture to dry the floor. The middle of the day is the best time to put your tent away because there may be moisture in the air in the early morning and late afternoon that will dampen the fabric enough to start the growth of mildew. (If you are forced to pack a wet tent when leaving camp, open it up and dry it out as soon as you reach home. Nylon tents are not so subject to mildew as are those made of canvas.)

Carefully brush off any leaves, twigs, dust, etc. before rolling it up loosely and putting it away in a cool, dry place.
Keep it in a tight-fitting tent bag only when transporting it
to and from camp. Otherwise, creases may damage the
fabric.

**No shoes, please!** No matter where you set up your tent, at
home and in camp, when you go inside pretend you're Ori-
entals and take off your shoes. If you don't, your cloth floor
won't retain it's waterproofing very long and it will soon
get holes in it.

**Some Other Don'ts:** Don't wet the canvas of the tent with
insect spray, because some of them will destroy the waterproofing. Nor should you use cleaning fluid on the tent for
the same reason. Remove dirt with a sponge dampened in
cool, clear water.

## Shovels

You should always take a shovel when you go camping. You
may need it for trenching around your tent, and there are
many other things around camp you may need it for: dig-
ging a latrine, building a campfire and then putting it out, or
helping put out a fire someone else's carelessness may have
started.

Your shovel doesn't have to be long-handled and awkward
to pack. There are efficient ones both that act as pick and
shovel and that fold up into an overall length of around
27 inches.

## Backpacks

The word "backpack" is used in two ways by hikers, campers, rock and mountain climbers. If they say they are "going
on a backpacking trip," they mean they will be marching off
somewhere with a pack on their back. But if they say

they're "going to carry a backpack," they can mean one of three things:

**Knapsacks:** These are small backpacks that hang from the shoulders without benefit of a frame to distribute their load. The full weight lies somewhere in the vicinity of the shoulder blades. Knapsacks are meant to carry no more than 20 pounds. The heavier the load, the more you'll find yourself leaning forward. Some have one, two or three pockets on the back and sides; some have none.

You can get by with a knapsack on a two-day camping trip provided you're not going to hike too far or too long, but we wouldn't recommend it for more than a one-day outing. In fact, knapsacks also are called "day packs."

Knapsacks range in approximate cost from $3 to $25, depending upon the materials from which they're made, who makes them and the quality of the workmanship, where you live, and the type of store or mail-order house from which you buy one.

**Rucksack:** This medium-sized pack, with a load limit of 40 pounds, is made to carry all the gear that one person needs on a one- or two-night camping trip. They are constructed on a built-in frame of aluminum, fiberglass or some other synthetic material and, together with a waist strap to keep the load from shifting, maintain their center of gravity nicely while walking. However, like the knapsack, the load is still suspended mainly from the shoulders and so a rucksack has its limitations.

They are available with from one to four pockets and with crescent-shaped metal hoops that make it possible for you to tie a bedroll to either top or bottom. The price ranges from $10 to $50.

**Packframes and Packsacks:** The frames are made of tubular aluminum, contoured to fit the body from shoulder to hips, and come in a variety of sizes to fit any physique. The sack is fitted onto the frame and, if held in place by a waist strap, will enable the hiker to carry just about any weight load within his physical limitations.

The contoured frame is engineered so that the load is distributed between shoulders and hips, with the weight mainly shifted to the strongest muscles of the body—legs, fanny, pelvis. Thus a person that's physically up to it can walk all day in normal upright position, the center of gravity remaining where it belongs.

These packs generally come with four or five outside pockets and with additional lashing and frame extensions to permit half again as much load for such bulky items as sleeping bags and fishing rods. As a general rule, the simpler they are, the better.

The cost: from $20 to $50.

Packframes and sacks are made in small, medium, large and extra-large sizes and here's how to tell which is for you:

| HEIGHT | MALE | FEMALE |
|---|---|---|
| Under 5'3" | small | small |
| 5'3" | medium* | small |
| 5'4" | medium | medium* |
| 5'5" | medium | medium |
| 5'6" | medium | medium |
| 5'7" | medium** | medium |
| 5'8" | large | medium*** |
| 5'9" | large | large |
| 5'10" | large | large |
| 5'11" | large | large |
| 6' | large**** | large |
| Over 6' | extra large | extra large |

\* Small if you're slightly built and will be carrying small, light loads.
\*\* Large if you're slightly built and will carry large, heavy loads.
\*\*\* Large if you're on the heavy side and will carry large, heavy loads.
\*\*\*\* Extra large if you're heavy and will carry large, heavy loads.

When choosing a backpack, perhaps more so than with any other camping equipment, it is important to have the guidance of a reputable outfitter.

## Bicycle and Motorcycle Panniers

You all know what saddlebags are, if not from firsthand experience, then certainly from watching Western movies. That is what a pannier is—a saddlebag, but shaped like an oblong box and with a thin sheet of plywood backing one side to keep the bag itself from rubbing against the wheel spokes. They come in pairs, allowing one to hang down on either side of the wheel.

They come in two sizes: large and small. The large fits over the rear wheel, the small over the front; the latter is meant to carry only very light loads so as not to foul up the wheel's maneuverability. The large pannier measures about 18 inches across, 14 inches in height and six inches in width. Dimensions of the small pannier are 12" x 8" x 4."

Load gear into panniers much as you would into backpacks, which we talk about next.

## What to Pack Along and How to Pack It

You may have seen lists of backpacking gear for a guy and a gal on a weekend camping trip on which the total weight adds up to about 27 or 28 pounds for the two of them. But you should remember when looking at such lists of equipment that it is probably the most modern, lightweight and expensive that money can buy. And the food to be taken along is probably freeze-dried only, which also is very expensive.

So you should probably figure that that same guy and gal might, between them, be just as apt to load their backpacks with anywhere from the ideal total of 27 or 28 pounds on up to two times or more that amount. Once they've learned all the things they can do without, they may be able to cut down that total load without undergoing any hardships.

For example, it's nice to have a roof over your head at night if it rains. But if it doesn't, it's much nicer to look at the stars. So if you're going where there's little danger of rain, you may be willing to gamble and get along without even so much as a lightweight backpacker's tent. However, you should take along at least a poncho (raincoats do not fit over backpacks); then, if it should rain, you can cover yourself with it. Or with a little ingenuity and some line, you can fashion a lean-to from it. Or take along a lightweight plastic tarp and make a lean-to from that (see page 74). If you don't have the protection of a tent you may want a mosquito netting cover.

Other than food enough to carry you through your stay in camp (see the section on foods in this book, paying particular attention to what we have to say about dried foods), here's a list of the essentials that you might have with you on any backpacking trip:

*Map, waterproof matches, sleepwear, extra socks and undergarments, extra shoelaces, first-aid kit (see page 62), snakebite kit, sunburn lotion, poncho, compass, one or two canteens of water, water-purification tablets, backpackers' stove and fuel, cooking and mess kits, can opener, a good pocket knife, nylon cord, backpacker's tarp and/or tent, toilet kit, needles and thread, toilet paper, flashlight, insect repellent, backpackers' grate, axe or folding saw, sleeping bag or bedroll, ground cloth, backpacker's mattress, survival kit.*

We have emphasized throughout this book that beginning campers should stay away from wilderness country unless they go with experienced campers or trained guides (see page 32). But no matter how safe you may think your trip will be, take along a small survival kit as a little added insurance and to help you form the habit for future, more hazardous trips. It should contain some nylon fishing line, two hooks and a fly, snare wire and additional water-purification tablets and waterproof matches.

Add to that whatever your heart desires so long as you don't mind hiking along with the extra weight.

Oh, yes, if you've got young ones going along who are big enough to keep up with you, buy each of them an appropriate pack and they should be able to carry a share of the load.

When two or more go backpacking, there are some things every person may not need to carry. So the added poundage as the size of the party increases can be reduced.

Once you've collected all your supplies, the thing to do is:

• Follow the suggestions on page 113 for removing dry foods from boxes that are bulky or have corners that may dig into you, measuring out what you need and repackaging in small, strong plastic bags.

• Roll your extra clothes so they'll pack individually into a minimal amount of space.

• Roll your extra socks and put them inside your moccasins if you should happen to be taking a pair along to serve as camp slippers and thus give your feet a respite from your heavier, more confining hiking boots.

• Group similar items together in easy-to-identify ditty bags.

• In other words, make everything as compact as possible so as to conserve space in your pack.

Now for the stowing. Here are some suggestions, but just to get you started experimenting to see what is best for you and your equipment. You should practice loading and unloading your pack several times before actually packing for a trip. And you should try walking with the pack on your back for a half mile or so.

One important thing to avoid is packing heavy items on the back of your pack so that their weight pulls you over backward and forces your body to tire itself compensating for the strain.

The center of gravity runs along your spine, through your legs and down to the ground.

• Heavy items should be packed high on your back and closest to your body. Medium-weight items next and lightest items farthest away from your body.

• Water canteens go in the upper side-pockets of your pack.

• The sleeping bag can be lashed to the bottom of your packsack if it won't fit inside, or, if you are carrying a rucksack, around its top and sides like a horseshoe.

• Your poncho goes in the topmost back pocket, so that you can get it in a hurry if a sudden shower catches you on the trail.

• Along-the-way snack items, such as nuts, raisins and other dried fruit, go in whatever pocket is handiest on your pack. So too with maps and compass, but perhaps you'd rather carry some of these items in your clothing pockets. It's up to you and the type of pack you have.

You'll notice that we've suggested nothing to dangle from your belt or from one of the many loops with which your pack may be fitted. Nor is there anything hanging from your shoulders but your pack.

One pair of straps is enough for any man, woman or child to sling over his shoulders—and now that we think of it, that pair should be padded for extra comfort. Some packs come with padded shoulder straps, some do not. If not, the store that sold you the pack also will sell you the pads.

Happy hiking.

### STORAGE BAGS

Storage bags, be they called "stuff," "duffel," "ditty" or "carry bags," are available in all shapes and sizes. Some are made of water-repellent canvas, some of plastic or water-proofed fabric (these, of course, are the thing to get for boat camping) and some (mainly for backpacking because they are so lightweight) of nylon. Some have metal grommets around the top through which to run a line; some have an ordinary drawstring; some have a convenient zipper on the side.

Before buying any of these bags, determine everything that you will be carrying and what sizes and shapes of bags this load will best fit into. Blankets and pillows can be rolled inside a light plastic tarpaulin (an old shower curtain or plastic tablecloth does very well), so you probably won't need special bags for them.

Don't figure on jamming everything you have into one or two huge bags; rather, divide things by category and pack them separately. Sometimes you can buy different colored bags to help you keep the bathing suits, for instance, separate from the sleepwear.

Although storage bags make packing and loading the car easy, as well as helping you keep your things neat and dry and clean at camp—and sometimes serve as hassocks for sitting—they are expendable when you first start camping. You can get by with old suitcases, airline bags, pillow cases (colored ones if possible), cardboard boxes and laundry bags. For small things that have to be kept dry, you can save the plastic bags in which produce is placed in some supermarkets. Use two of them for additional strength and fasten with a rubber band. So, if funds are limited, put storage bags at the bottom of the list to buy sometime in the future. With one exception, and that's bags for such things as flour or cereal that you take backpacking. For these things spend a little money and buy a type of plastic bag that's not likely to leak or break.

## Portable Toilet

As we've pretty well established by now, going to the bathroom at most modern campgrounds is as simple as walking a short distance from your tent to the public facility. You may want to take along disposable paper seat covers (you can buy them by the package at your camping-goods store) just in case they're not supplied by the management. Some of the least-improved campgrounds give you an idea of what it was like going to the bathroom in days of old by providing the good old-fashioned outhouse, sometimes known as a "Chic Sale." Here, too, you'll probably want to have a disposable paper seat cover.

Maybe you don't feel at ease on the wooden seat of a "Chic Sale" or maybe your children are frightened by it or your grandma is too arthritic to make the walk to the modern bathhouse or maybe you'll pitch your tent somewhere in the outback where there are no improvements whatsoever. Whatever the problem, there's a very up-to-date solution. Buy a portable toilet. If you didn't know there were such things, go to the closest good-sized camping outfitter and look them over.

One is a chemically operated affair that closely resembles your john at home. The big difference is that it can be flushed from 40 to 60 times before it needs to be emptied because the chemical breaks down the solids in the wastes and also makes them odorless. Which means you might be able to get by for the entire weekend and take it home for emptying into a regular toilet. You can buy one that weighs about 25 pounds, plus the weight of the five gallons of water that go into it, which would add approximately another 40 pounds, making a total of 65. The price: $80 to $90.

The other type of portable john is much cheaper. It sells for about $6. It's a regular toilet seat with folding legs, commonly called by the trade name of "Safari Toilet." You suspend a strong plastic bag (they come by the package) underneath the seat. Use one bag for each sitting, remove and fasten with a wire twist. You should check with the campground management or park officials as to where they should be dumped.

# Chapter 3

# Lanterns, Heaters, Stoves, Coolers and Other Cooking and Eating Equipment

### General Information about Lanterns, Heaters and Stoves

Lanterns, heaters and stoves fueled by gasoline have been favorites among campers for many years. They are economical to operate, the fuel is easy to obtain and gives off a hot heat and a bright light. Though still popular with many, they have some drawbacks. They have to be pumped and primed, and the highly combustible gasoline fuel must be poured into them. The parts, especially if leaded gasoline is used in error, sometimes require tinkering with.

Propane equipment, which is simpler to use than its gasoline-operated counterparts (the stoves work just like a kitchen gas stove) has been coming more and more into use since camping has become a family affair. As a matter of fact, so popular is propane equipment that you can buy a unit which will convert a gasoline stove to propane.

Propane (and butane) gas is a liquid petroleum (sometimes referred to as LPG), which remains a liquid only while being held under pressure in storage. Propane camping equipment fuel comes either in disposable cylinders or in a refillable bottle, which makes the gas considerably cheaper than in the cylinders. The bottle can be hooked up to a stove by a leakproof hose; one or two other appliances (refrigerator, lantern, heater or propane barbecue) can also be attached to the container at the same time.

You'll find some equipment operated by fuels other than gasoline or propane, and you may want to look it over and discuss its merits with a qualified outfitter and other campers before you buy. But the two big camp equipment fuels as of this writing are white gasoline (which is often confusingly referred to as "gas") and propane gas.

Refinements and changes are constantly being made, and new manufacturers are coming into the picture to give the well-known old-timers some stiff competition. So keep your eyes open for new developments.

Before deciding on a particular piece of equipment, compare it with other models. Here are some of the features to look into:

• How much heat or light will it generate? Power may be measured in BTUs (British thermal units). Sixty-four hundred BTUs is sufficient for any camp cooking purposes.

• Is power adjustable? The power on all new stoves and lanterns is probably adjustable, but on some heaters it must remain fixed at one temperature, which can be a distinct disadvantage.

• How much does it weigh compared with other models? This is an important factor in backpacking, bicycle camping, etc.

• What is the lowest temperature at which it will operate efficiently?

• Can the fuel container be removed from the rest of the assembly before it is empty?

• Are couplings standard?

• Will it fold up into a case that's easy to pack and that will protect the more delicate parts?

It is most important that equipment operated by a fuel of any kind be of good quality.

Here are some precautions to help prevent accidents from happening when using lanterns, heaters and stoves:

• Don't light pieces of equipment on which you must use a match, or that might flare up, inside a tent. Light them outside and carry them in.

• Be sure, if using them inside, that the tent is well ventilated, not only because flame eats up the oxygen but also to get rid of any fumes that might leak out of a faulty piece of equipment. To avoid the latter, read all instructions, follow them exactly and keep the equipment in top-notch working order.

• Never change fuel cylinders or pour liquid fuel while the lantern, heater or stove is hot or near a campfire, and don't throw the empty cartridge into the campfire. Keep your campfire and your camp-stove operation far enough removed from each other for safety.

• Never pour gasoline inside a tent or any other enclosure, and if you spill any, wait for all fumes to evaporate (and screw the cap back on the container) before striking a match.

• The gasoline used for camp equipment should always be the white, nonleaded kind, and the kind that is sold especially for this purpose is the best kind to buy. Gasoline should be stored only in clearly marked red cans so there can be no mistake about the substance they contain. This is especially important where the white gasoline is concerned, because it has no odor and looks like water.

• All fuels should be stored at camp outside the tent, in the shade and at a safe distance from the campfire site.

• Never place a lantern, heater or camp stove where it will touch the walls or ceiling of your tent, sleeping bag or anything else that could either flame, scorch or melt.

## Lanterns and Other Camp Lights

Flashlights are a must when you go camping. There should be one for each group of sleepers, one in the car or station wagon and another in the tent for whoever may be sleeping there. Then, if the children are startled by the unaccustomed sound of a cricket chirping, they can reassure themselves safely by flicking on the switch of their flashlight. Or they can use it to awaken Mommy or Daddy to take them to the bathroom.

Not only can you take along flashlights to dissipate safely

and quickly the shadows from tent corner or forest path, but electric lanterns are available now, too.

Backpackers often get by with a tiny flashlight and/or a small folding lantern made for holding a specially made candle, than which you can buy no cheaper fuel.

Although there is nothing more helpful and cheery than a good propane or gasoline lantern to light up your campsite while you cook and eat, there's no reason why you shouldn't be able to get by without one until you can afford to buy a good one. Just see to it that you cook and eat before dark, unless, of course, you are camping where you can have a campfire to add warmth and light.

When you do invest in a lantern, be it for your first trip or your twenty-first, be sure you get one with a solid base that won't tip over easily and a handle by which it can be hung up.

## Heaters

There are good heaters available, but you should not need to invest in one until you have had a good deal of experience and go in for cold-weather camping. If and when you do buy, your safest bet will be the one that operates by a "catalytic" process. This type is engineered so that the surface doesn't give off too much heat, which means you won't easily burn yourself on one, and if a piece of clothing falls on the heater, it won't catch on fire. Propane catalytic heaters do not flame up when being lit as do the gasoline models.

## Stoves

Camp stoves are playing more of a leading role in camp cooking and for very good reasons:

1. With so many people camping, loose dry wood is, except in wilderness areas and on some beaches, becoming harder and harder to find.

2. When the woods are tinder dry, you will often not be

permitted to build a fire, sometimes not even with charcoal. You should find out when you enter your camping area what the regulations are at that particular time and place.

The more people use camp stoves, the more they realize how much more convenient they are than a campfire when all they want is a quick cup of coffee or bowl of canned soup.

You may find that the ideal arrangement for you for a big meal is to cook the meat and maybe bake the potatoes tastily over either a wood-burning campfire or a charcoal fire while cooking the other things on a camp stove.

We tell you on page 152 how to build a campfire that is a combination heartwarming, sit-around one as well as a cooking fire. It's called the "keyhole lay."

*We'd better mention here, so you'll be sure to take it along, that the instrument you should use to cut most of your firewood is a saw—not the oft-pictured axe.* Why? For the very simple reason that a saw is more efficient and far less dangerous to its user than is an axe. We like one that is shaped roughly like a triangle and is made especially for campers. If you do take an axe, be sure it's a sharp one. A sharp axe bites into the chunk of wood while a dull one is apt to glance off and bite into your leg!

If you buy a camp stove, reread our general comments on what to look for when buying camp equipment. Get one that has a windshield, and also look for a model that's easy to clean.

We like a two-burner stove and when we're going to do a lot of cooking, an additional one-burner stove. We find this a better arrangement than having one big three-burner unit. It's easier for two people to help with the cooking when the two units are separated, and sometimes it's hard to fit three good-sized pots and pans on three burners. (Better measure the utensils you will be using on it before buying your stove.)

There's another reason for having a one-burner stove. If you get the right kind, it can do double duty for backpacking. So when you buy it, look over the stoves specially designed for that purpose. It would be wise to get the advice of an outfitter who really knows the backpacking business.

If outdoor cooking is one of the reasons you go camping,

then you should take a look at the fold-up stovetop ovens
available for use over the burners of a camp stove. There's
also a reflector oven to be had which works fairly well at the
edge of a campfire if you want to bake. We'll say no more
about ovens in this book, though, since most overnight or
weekend campers don't want to go to quite that much
trouble. However, we do tell you in the recipe section how
to bake biscuits in a heavy pot.

Try out your stove (or stoves) at home two or three times
before going to camp. Your camping trip will be more fun if
you already are at ease with your stove.


## Grate (or Grille)

If you are going to do any cooking over coals, either wood or
charcoal, take along a grate (sometimes called "grille") to
lay over them. We sometimes borrow a shelf from our
kitchen oven. But for backpacking you'll want something
very small and of a shape that will fit into your pack.

You can use the grate over a slit trench as well as over the
keyhole-lay campfire.

You may also want a good-sized long-handled hinged grille
to hold steaks, chops, hamburgers and fish firmly so you can
handle and turn them over easily.


## Charcoal Cookers

You can always take along a charcoal cooker with folding
legs. Most people with yards or porches have them, but if
you do not, you can buy one for just a few dollars. If you buy
one, be sure to get one with a grate that raises and lowers
easily and that comes completely off.

You may want to take a look at Primus' Campecue, which
resembles a charcoal cooker with a layer of what looks like
charcoal in the firebed but which actually is lava rock. It does
not burn as does charcoal but is heated by a cylinder of
propane. The principle is the same as for the gas cookers

that have been springing up in people's yards the past three years or so. You cook on this type of stove just the same way as if you were using charcoal and the meat looks and tastes as if it had been cooked over hot coals, but you don't have to keep replacing the coals. You replace the propane cylinder instead. The grease on the coals can be burned off simply by turning heat up to maximum. The cooker will run for four hours on any standard disposable cylinder or it can be hooked up to operate from any large refillable bottle. The Campecue folds up into a neat and convenient carrying case.

You can buy a good two-burner camp stove for anywhere from $20 to $40. There's no exact way to say, but it would probably cost you at least twice as much to eat meals of comparable quality in restaurants as to prepare them outdoors. Which means that, even if you buy a stove and/or a charcoal cooker, you'd be ahead of the game before many weekends were over if not having them meant you'd do your eating in restaurants.

## The Auto Fire Charcoal Lighter

Whatever the type of charcoal cooker you use, of utmost importance is the way you start the charcoal you put in it. Just one glance at the warnings on charcoal lighter fluid cans should be enough to convince you the fluid method is *not* the way. We are happy to say we found the right way and we'll be even happier to pass the good word along to you. You don't need electricity, there's no chemical flavor or smell, and your coals are ready to cook over in an unbelievably short time.

The name of this charcoal lighter is the Auto Fire and it looks like a piece of stovepipe with holes around the bottom. Set it in your charcoal stove, put a wad of newspaper under the trapdoor just above the row of holes and pour inexpensive charcoal briquets into the upper part. Now stick a lighted match through the holes until the wadded paper catches fire. Wait until the charcoal is starting to turn hot pink and gray, then open the trapdoor, spilling the coals into your stove, adjust your grate to fit about four inches above them and start cooking. It's so quick and simple most people don't believe us, but if you buy one, you'll discover we're telling the truth on your first try. If you can't find one (many department stores now carry them), write to the manufacturer: G. B. Byars, President, The Auto Fire Corporation, P.O. Box 487, Corinth, Mississippi 38834. The price, postpaid, is $5.95 for an aluminized one, $9.95 for the stainless-steel version.

The Auto Fire, in addition to starting charcoal, can be used as a cookstove or even a heater. Set a frying pan containing bacon and eggs or the fish you just caught over the top as soon as enough heat comes from the charcoal, and you're in business.

## The Stove for Boat Camping

In the "Boat Camping" section we tell you to set up camp along a river or lake bank or on an island just the same as you would in a camp anywhere else. Use any of the stoves we have described, but do not, we repeat *do not use* them aboard your boat. Carry them along with the fuel, but wait until you get ashore to set them up and light them. Only boats with built-in kitchens are safe to cook aboard.

If you buy such a boat, you will be interested to know that the safest boat-cooking fuels are, in order: electricity, coal, coke or wood, canned heat, alcohol, kerosene and liquid petroleum gas (propane or butane). Gasoline is so dangerous to use on a boat that it's not even on the list.

## Fire Extinguisher

Anyone who uses fire, including people who camp, should always keep a fire extinguisher close by. We urge you to acquire a dry-chemical all-purpose extinguisher and to take it along with you on every camping trip. They are effective both indoors and out on any kind of fire no matter what the source: gasoline, grease, wood, electric appliances, paint. They are as easy to use as any aerosol spray. Just aim, press and that's it. Such an extinguisher is good to have around the house, so it won't be money wasted.

Here's hoping you'll never have to use it. And you won't, if you'll only remember what Smokey the Bear has to say about taking extra care.

## Tables and Chairs

You can buy a folding camp table on which to set most camp stoves, and, believe us, it's easier cooking on a table than squatting on your haunches or bending over. But an improved campground will be almost certain to have a good-sized camp table with benches at every campsite, and you can set your stove right on that table. (A few stoves might need a sheet of asbestos under them.) Just take a glance at your campground directory under the column headed "Tables" (listed under "Facilities").

If you're going to an unimproved camp, you're going to want some kind of table you can easily carry. When going to a beach by boat, we've sometimes taken along two or three metal lap trays with short folding legs. They fold up into fairly convenient carrying sizes and aren't bad to eat from when you're sitting on the sand, a piece of driftwood or a ledge the water has obligingly carved. These trays aren't bad to use while sitting in the car either, if you're going to drive to your campsite and don't want to take along camp chairs and a folding table.

Sometimes you can utilize a couple of wooden boxes and a board to make a table. Don't hesitate to use your ingenuity, because only you can know the circumstances under which you will be camping.

There will be times, of course, such as when you're backpacking or when space is at a premium in a small boat, that both tables and chairs will be out of the question, and the most you can hope to carry with you is a small piece of waterproof material to set your dishes and food on to keep them clean.

As we said, there are picnic tables with benches at most improved campground sites, so if you are headed for one of them, you probably won't want to bother taking additional things to sit on just for an overnight or weekend camping trip. If, however, you intend spending most of your time sitting around camp, eating and socializing, then the picture changes. First consider folding yard chairs. If you don't have any, take a look at camp chairs, which may be smaller and less bulky. Try them before buying to see if they are comfortable, and, whatever you do, don't buy such cheap ones that they fall apart after a couple of sittings!

## Pots, Pans and Other Eating Equipment

Nesting sets of pots and pans look beautiful in the store, but stop and think a minute before you buy them. Are they made of the type and weight of material that through years of trial and error in the kitchen has become your choice? The odds against it are pretty high. Unless you're going backpacking or bike camping, the additional weight of two or three pots and pans that you really enjoy cooking with generally won't make that much difference.

If you do decide to do any buying, unless it's for backpacking, give serious consideration to a Dutch oven, which is generally nothing more than a large pot made of heavy material that conducts and holds the heat well enough to bake in it. You may already have such a utensil in your kitchen.

We have heard of people who take their pressure cookers to camp to use on camp stoves on which the heat can be adjusted.

So look through what you have at home and see if you can't do a fair job of making up a set of pots and pans from equipment you already have. We discovered that we could make our own nest by setting a five-quart heavy aluminum pot inside a large, heavy iron frying pan. Inside the pot went a mixing bowl, inside the bowl a small, heavy aluminum pot, inside the small pot some hot-pot lifters, over that a small round wire rack, then the two pot lids.

Add a coffee pot (you can use it for heating water as well as making coffee), and that's more than enough pots and pans for some pretty fancy weekend cooking for any family. You will want to coordinate the pots and pans you take along with the kind of things you expect to cook or vice versa. Whether you put the cart before the horse or the egg before the chicken, just be sure you have a trial run or two at home, using your camp stove and/or charcoal stove, the pots and pans and other kitchen utensils you intend taking to camp, *and* practice on the menus you expect to prepare.

If you are going backpacking, it's doubly important that you decide your menus before packing your cooking dishes. You may find that you can get by with just one lightweight pot that you can use for both cooking and heating dishwater. Plus, of course, a bare minimum of eating utensils.

Something you may want to check into if buying cooking and eating equipment for backpacking is plastic tubes designed to hold honey and such. You fill them, then squeeze out the amount you want to use.

Perhaps even more important than practicing cooking with camp equipment is trying your hand at dishwashing without benefit of an electric dishwasher or even hot and cold running water. Be sure you figure on enough pots for heating boiling-hot water for both washing and rinsing the dishes. If you leave any soap on them, you and your family may as well pack up and go home, because it can give you very unpleasant stomach cramps and diarrhea!

Here are some dishwashing suggestions:
• It will make it easier to wash the smoke stains off pots and pans if, before cooking over coals (either wood or charcoal), you coat the outside of the pots and pans with yellow soap.
• It will make dishwashing a lot easier if, immediately after eating, you use paper towels to wipe dishes, silverware, pots and pans as clean of food as possible.
• You will also find dishwashing easier if you take along plenty of steel-wool pads, the ones filled with soap.

While we're talking about washing dishes, we'd better mention that you'll need a bucket of some kind for carrying water. Even if you go to an improved campground, you'll need one. You can get some kind of a collapsible bucket or you can use a large cooking pot with a bail-type handle. You can also use it for heating water or cooking, too. As we've said so many times before, try to get by at first with things you have at home, then, after a little exposure to camp conditions and firsthand experience, you'll have a better idea what *you* will find most suitable.

All of the other equipment you need—dishes, silverware, knives, forks, spoons, spatulas, etc.—for cooking, you should be able to requisition from your supplies at home; just be sure that you add them all to your list and don't forget to take them along.

## Portable Coolers, Vacuum Jars and Water Carriers
## and the Importance of Camp Refrigeration

If you want to include such perishables as fresh meat, milk, butter and eggs in your camp menus, there is no other single piece of equipment so important as a camp cooler. Why? We'll let the U.S. Public Health Service speak for us by excerpting from its booklet, *No Picnic*:

Disease-producing bacteria prefer certain types of food, particularly those high in protein and moisture—such as milk, milk products, eggs, meat, poultry, fish, shellfish—and such products as cream pies, custards and potato salad. For this reason, we refer to these types of food as potentially hazardous. These foods must be kept either hot or cold.

Hot is 140° F. or above. Cold is 40° F. or below. Temperatures between 40° F. and 140° F. are unsafe. Disease-producing bacteria grow most rapidly at the middle of this temperature range.

If you have little or no facilities for maintaining these foods hot or cold, DO NOT TAKE THEM! Instead, plan your picnics (or other outings) around canned, preserved or dehydrated food, fresh fruits and vegetables.

Do not refrigerate in deep containers. Food acts as an insulator and the center of large masses can be warm for long periods of time though the outer edges may be almost frozen. Use shallow pans and fill no more than three to four inches deep.

Remember, refrigeration does not kill disease-producing bacteria. It only slows their growth.

Cover the serving area (ground, blanket or table) with a tablecloth to provide a clean surface on which to place food. Food should be kept covered except when being prepared or served.

Return leftover potentially hazardous food to the ice-chest immediately after the meal. If there is no ice left, or the food has been at an unsafe temperature for long meal periods, THROW IT OUT! The best plan is to limit food quantities so there will be no leftovers. Don't make the mistake of serving foods at lunchtime, then leaving them unrefrigerated to serve again later in the day.

We hope, after reading this excerpt from the Public Health Service's booklet, you'll agree that you shouldn't buy the cheapest cooler you can find. Follow the government's suggestion and use nonperishable foods until you can afford a good cooler (with care, it will last a long time), then buy from a reliable camp outfitter.

A cooler's insulation should be a good synthetic; urethane at this writing seems to be the best, with polystyrene foam running a close second. The exterior material, if it will be banged about, should be good-quality metal. Metal also increases the insulating ability of a cooler.

Coolers come in many shapes and sizes. Some stand on their sides, some on their ends, and some are reversible. So, if you first decide how much you will need to carry in it (is baby's formula going along, for instance?) and *where* in the car you want to carry it, you shouldn't have too much trouble finding the right box for you.

We, for instance, have a cooler that's roughly 13" x 13" x 22" which fits exactly between our front and back seats. It has a top opening, so when we stop at a roadside picnic table for lunch (or if in an emergency we want to eat a sandwich without stopping), we can lift off the lid and get what we want without bothering to open the trunk or removing the ice chest from the car (and the cold air, which sinks, stays on the bottom of the chest).

There are several things you should check for besides the material from which a camp cooler is made:

• If the dimensions permit it, a shelf on which to set a

block of ice. The shelf (again if dimensions don't interfere) should permit the ice to be placed in the top and/or middle of the box, as cold air settles downward. The ideal arrangement is to have some sort of container in which to put the ice so it doesn't fill your chest with water as it melts.

• Interior corners should be rounded for easy cleaning.

• Doors or lids should seal tightly when closed, but check on new childproof latches, designed to keep children from locking themselves in empty coolers.

• It should have an adequate drainage system.

• The box should have fixed handles for easy carrying. Stay away from any that have removable handles.

• It should have a stainproof and rustproof interior.

Don't try to get along with a cooler that's too small to allow you room for a sufficient supply of ice. Many weekend campers find an 11-gallon box about right for their needs. A good one can be purchased for about $20.

We freeze our ice (sometimes we use fruit juice and drink it as it melts) in plastic containers in order to avoid a mess. Some people freeze their own ice in quart and half-gallon milk cartons. A chunk of ice keeps much longer than do ice cubes weighing an equal amount. If you do buy ice cubes and you have no container in which to put them, add them to the cooler while still enclosed in the plastic bag in which they usually come from campground stores or service-station coin machines. They'll last much longer—and will be less messy—than if you sprinkle them around loose. We sometimes put one ice container in a soft insulated plastic zipper bag, put the bag inside the cooler and store our most perishable things, such as meat, in the bag. That way it's protected from the warm air that rushes in whenever the cover of the cooler is removed, as well as being surrounded by a double insulation.

You will get the most from the cold air you have if you can manage to load the most perishable foods in the bottom of the cooler, where it will be the coldest, and things such as bread, fruits and vegetables—things that you only want to be cool so they'll stay fresh—on top.

You will have to devise a system that is best for you and the ice chest you have. But be sure to check your system out to see if it maintains food at safe temperatures. It's very simple. Just fill your cooler with ice and *chilled* food, then proceed to use the food just as if you were on a camping trip. That way you can see how long the ice will last in the freezing containers you have.

Get a refrigerator thermometer and test the temperature in different areas of the chest. It's a good idea to leave the thermometer there even when you go to camp. It will remind you how quickly the temperature of your box rises (and, of course, how quickly the ice will melt) when you open the door or take off the cover more than is absolutely necessary. With a little experimenting, you'll soon learn where and how to place your ice and how much of it you'll need to get maximum efficiency from your cooler.

Besides using plastic ice containers, another way to avoid the mess of melting ice in your chest is not to use ice but to invest in freezer jells. They are a jelly-like substance that is sealed in plastic and can be refrozen in your home freezer and then reused in your camp cooler. Test them in your cooler so you'll be sure you're carrying enough to keep perishables at the correct temperature.

Your ice (be it made from water or fruit juice or even freezer jells) and your food will last longer if you do this:

Put a large container of ice in your cooler, close it and let it stand that way overnight just before packing it to go camping. Thoroughly chill all foods, including fruits and vegetables, that will go into the box. (They should be under 40° F.).

When you get to camp, store your cooler in a cool, shady place. Throw a tarp over it for double insulation and keep melted ice water drained off.

One last word: If you keep perishables beyond the evening of your second day, you'll probably have to replace melted ice with a fresh supply.

## VACUUM JARS

Vacuum jars can be used for a lot more than just carrying cold drinks or hot coffee. For example, your first day's lunch at camp can come out of them! Here's how: Just before leaving home, heat a precooked goulash or stew-type pot of food to boiling (put the lid on and let it simmer awhile so all chunks are thoroughly heated), pour it into one or more vacuum jars that have been preheated with boiling water and quickly seal. Then you're all set for a hot lunch when you arrive in camp without even lighting a match!

Just one precaution. If you'll look back at page 104, you'll note that the Public Health Service cautions us that "hot is 140° F. or above." So you want to be sure your food when you open the vacuum jar will meet that health requirement. Long before going to camp test your jar with similar food and a food thermometer (you can stick the prong of a meat thermometer into the contents). The better quality your jar, the longer your food will retain heat. Don't depend on a large picnic jug designed for cold drinks to keep food at the recommended hot temperature. We have a four-cup vacuum jar in which a stew will remain above 140° F. for 12 hours, which means we can fill the jar with boiling food at seven in the morning, drive two hours to camp, spend the rest of the morning doing whatever we like and still sit down to a nice hot bowl of stew around noon without taking time to cook. According to Mrs. Doris V. Erickson, Nassau County Leader of New York State Cooperative Extension Service, we could keep that jar full of perishable food until dinner if it contained plenty of acid such as tomato or wine. Without the acid content, she advises, don't hold hot perishable foods in vacuum jars for longer than four or five hours even though they stay at 140° F. or above.

*Vacuum Jar of Boiling Water:* If four people in a family like four different hot drinks for lunch, either along the road or when you get to camp, do this: Take along a four-cup vacuum jar of boiling water and individual portions of instant mix for whatever each person wants: coffee, tea, bouillon, cocoa, maybe even a dehydrated soup.

WATER CARRIERS

We always carry a two-quart insulated jug that starts out about half-filled with ice and half with water, and a stack of paper cups in a plastic bag. You can buy jugs that are bigger, but we find the two-quart size much easier to handle in a moving car. If two quarts aren't enough for your family, instead of buying one huge, unwieldy container, we recommend getting two of the two-quart size. Fill one with juice or punch or iced tea and one with water. Make ice cubes of whatever drink you are carrying, then they won't dilute it.

If ice isn't readily available, the best sort of container for drinking water is a desert water bag that you can hang on the side of the car. These are made of a tightly woven material that lets just enough water seep through so that constant evaporation keeps the contents of the bag cool.

If you must carry a large amount or all of your water with you (see "Water," page 114), we consider the best containers the five-gallon jerry cans of the type that are widely used in the military; next best are canteens and water jugs.

If you are going backpacking, canteens are now available in plastic as well as metal, and you may want to take a look at leather, plastic-lined wineskins. Consider how you will be carrying your water supply, what materials will keep it the coolest and the weight of the container when deciding which to buy. When hiking in hot country, some backpackers like the desert water bag we mentioned.

# Chapter 4

# Food (Including Recipes)

### About Perishable Foods

*If you didn't read the section on "Portable Coolers," etc. and the importance of camp refrigeration (pages 104 to 108), we suggest you do so before going any farther. We tell you there some very important things about the temperatures at which perishables must be kept.*

Buy your meats from a reputable butcher and try to get them (unless you're going to prefreeze them) the day before you leave. Milk, eggs and other perishables also should be of good quality and fresh.

Ground meat, that all-time favorite of outdoor cooks, is especially perishable because so much of its surface has had an opportunity to be exposed to contamination. We recommend it be used the same day you go to camp, and if possible, keep it even lower than 40° F. One way to do this is to prepare it ahead of time in easy-to-handle frozen patties this way: Shape your patties, spread them out on a cookie sheet in a single layer, cover with freezer paper and freeze. As soon as they are frozen solid, transfer them from the cookie sheet to a plastic freezer bag. Frozen this way, they won't stick together and can be easily removed from the bag and spread out on the grate over coals.

If you take ground meat in bulk to camp, try to start out with it partially frozen, just enough so it will be defrosted by the time you plan to use it. If you remove a package from the freezer—say one that's about one and a half to two inches thick—and leave it overnight in your refrigerator, then load it in your camp cooler the next morning, it will probably be defrosted enough to handle easily at camp that night. Test it out in your camp cooler at home and make any necessary changes in package thickness or timing.

Poultry, too, is quite perishable. If possible, eat it the same day you carry it to camp in your cooler, whether you carry it cooked or raw. It should always be cooked until well done and never partially cooked to be completed at a later time.

Steaks and chops, unless frozen, should if possible be used the same day you remove them from your home refrigerator. If frozen and stored properly in a good camp cooler, they will stay good and cold until the second or sometimes the third day. They should be cooked while they still retain a few ice crystals.

Salt-cured meats such as bacon and ham will keep well in your camp cooler at 40° F. or lower for a three-day weekend period. Frankfurters probably will, too, but it doesn't hurt to prefreeze them to be on the safe side.

We don't recommend carrying perishable organ meats with you to camp. If you do, be sure to freeze them first.

And we don't recommend that you carry fish with you, either. Catch it or buy it at your destination.

We feel there are certain foods frequently used by campers about which there is a good deal of misunderstanding when it comes to "should they" or "needn't they" be refrigerated. So we asked Mrs. Erickon if she could clear it up for us. Here's what she had to say:

Soft cheeses must be kept refrigerated at all times and kept in their original containers when possible because the original containers are sterile; storage life varies from three to five days up to two weeks. Spreads, once opened, keep one to two weeks. Hard cheeses should be kept under refrigeration and will keep two weeks to two months, depending upon freshness when purchased and the variety. A little mold can be cut off and the remainder used, but if cheese becomes very moldy, discard it, because yeasts may grow and make conditions favorable for bacteria, especially if the surface is moist.

Dried eggs will keep unopened for about a year if kept in a dry cool place (under 50° F.) preferably in the refrigerator. Once opened, they should be refrigerated, tightly covered and used within three days. Reconstituted egg solids should be used immediately or covered tightly, refrigerated and used within an hour. They should be used only in dishes that will be *thoroughly* cooked. You would have to go by package directions for freeze-dried egg solids.

Butter and margarine are all right as long as they stay firm.

Vegetable oils do not need to be kept refrigerated.

There's no hazard to eggs as long as the shell is intact (they should be discarded for even the slightest crack), but they should definitely be refrigerated. Eggs lose their quality very rapidly when left at room temperature. Hard-boiled eggs, on the other hand, are sterile products as long as the shell is intact and don't need to be refrigerated.

After cooking (or after the can is opened), low-acid vegetables such as corn, peas and beans should be kept refrigerated and used within three days.

She added this very important comment: "There are many types of food spoilage, some deadly, that look, smell and taste all right. I find that most people think otherwise."

## Dried Foods

There are a great many freeze-dried foods now available, just about anything you might want, including many kinds of meats and even, believe it or not, ice cream. Some people like these foods and others prefer something else. So before stocking up on them for a camping trip, we suggest you try a few at home. Test them for quantity as well as for taste. You may, after a day's hiking, consider what the packager presents as being sufficient for two as more suitable for one. Freeze-dried foods are so lightweight that unquestionably they are a boon for the backpacker.

Although in their dehydrated state perishable freeze-dried foods do not need refrigeration, they do as soon as liquid has been added to them. So if you are backpacking or bicycle camping or going in any other way that does not permit you to carry a cooler of any kind, throw away the leftovers. Don't try to carry them with you for the next meal.

Most camping-equipment stores don't carry a complete line of freeze-dried foods. If you don't find enough of an assortment, get the address of the processor from one of the packages and write for a complete price list and he will probably mail to you direct.

Besides the freeze-dried foods, there are other easy-to-carry dried foods that are sometimes suitable for campers—such things as dried fruits, nuts, rice and other cereal grains you can find at health-food stores, quick-cooking lentils (they are orange-colored) and even popcorn.

**Don't think that because you are getting away from it all you should also get away from good nutrition. It's just as important on a camping trip as any other time.**

So browse around in supermarkets to see what an interesting variety of dried fruits, proteins and cereal grains you can find, and don't overlook what is sometimes a very good source for these things, a health-food store. We give you on page 120 our very own recipe for granola, which includes dried fruit, coconut, nuts, and three different grains.

You will probably find it convenient, especially for backpacking, to premix dry ingredients in serving-size plastic packets (you can buy special heavy-duty kinds at camping-goods stores). Fasten securely with a rubber band each serving packet of coffee or tea, sugar and dry milk powder, candy or dried apples, prunes or apricots and nuts. You can put all the little packets in one medium-sized plastic or nylon bag.

You can also premeasure the amount of rice, lentils, etc. for a specific recipe, label it so you know *which* recipe, put in a small, tough plastic bag and fasten this container too with a rubber band.

Be imaginative and do as much of the work of handling and measuring before you leave home as possible.

Many people feel that the energy you get from sugar in dried fruit stays with you longer than that from candy. Whether you agree or not, the fruit is less messy in warm weather and contributes more nutritional variety.

## Water

While talking about nutrition, let's not overlook one of the most important substances of all: water.

The U.S. Air Force Survival Manual says that even in cold areas the human body needs two quarts of water a day to maintain efficiency. Of course, part of that two quarts can be in the form of another beverage. And we should point out that in hot weather and during strenuous activity, much more water may be required.

So wherever you are going, you must know that there will be water waiting for you (backpackers take heed) or you must carry it with you.

You can find out about the availability of water from U.S. Geological Survey maps. They can be obtained by writing to the U.S. Geological Survey, Washington, D.C., for maps of areas east of the Mississippi and to the Denver Federal Center, Denver, Colorado, for areas west of the Mississippi. You can also get this information by contacting the forest or park service or other agency in charge of the particular area where you expect to go.

Almost all commercial campgrounds and many improved public campgrounds have drinking water available, but, when checking on other things, it's a good idea to check on the drinking water, too. When you get to camp, just be sure you use water for drinking, cooking and dishwashing that is meant for those purposes or else purify it as described below.

Wilderness sites may have a stream or a lake or a spring from which you can get your water supply. If you are far enough from civilized man and his pollution, this water may be clean enough to drink, but you can never be sure. You cannot tell by appearance. So what do you do?

You purify it either by boiling it for a minimum of five

minutes or by adding three drops (six drops if the water is cloudy) of two percent tincture of iodine per quart of water and letting it stand for one hour, or by using water-purification tablets according to the instructions on the package.

Boiled water has a flat taste which can be improved by adding a bit of salt and by aerating it by pouring it back and forth between two clean containers.

Water from melted snow should be purified in the same way as any other water of questionable quality. You may find it more palatable (it lacks minerals) if you add tea.

There are few springs that are actually poisonous; however, if you should come across water around which there is no green vegetation or where bones of dead animals are scattered about, *don't use it.*

## Providing for Your Pet

If Fido or Puss is going to camp with you, you'll have to provide food that will not be upsetting. This means they should have the same food they've been eating at home—and the same dish they've been eating from.

## Buying Food Along the Way

If you are going to or passing by an area that has interesting food for sale, you may want to make your menus flexible enough so that you can include some of those foods. Take along enough nonperishable canned or dried foods, though, just in case you are disappointed.

Sometimes you may go camping at the end of the harvesting season, and a farmer will let you pick what you want for almost nothing just to help get rid of the tag end of the crop.

Learn to spot genuine farm stands. Some of them are just outlets for produce bought from other sources. Stands selling fruits and vegetables that look as if they came from the farm itself are usually the best bet. So you'd better learn to recognize an apple tree if you're buying apples, a cornfield if you're buying corn, etc.

## Planning Camp Menus

Unless you're willing to risk taking too much food and perhaps wasting it, or taking too little and going hungry, it's necessary to plan your menus even before you shop. Here are two ways to do it:

*The easiest but least satisfactory:* Roughly estimate a little less fresh food than you think you'll need, then take along enough additional canned or dried food to bolster it as needed.

*A better way to do it:*

• Decide what you will eat and drink at each meal and write it down.

• List the ingredients for each dish, showing the amount. We'd suggest you figure servings a little bigger than what you do at home. All that fresh air and exercise are going to whet appetites! This even means such things as butter (or margarine); estimated cups of tea, coffee or cocoa; and seasonings such as salt, pepper, sugar and catsup. Keep this list and use it whenever you want to repeat the same menu on a camping trip.

• Check your list of ingredients against the supplies you have on hand and buy what you don't have.

• As you pack your food supplies for the trip, check off each item on your list of ingredients to be sure it's included.

• Always plan on eating the most perishable foods first.

If you have toddlers who will be going with you who need watching, plan your menus so that almost all of your food preparation is done at home, or make do with ready-prepared foods that need nothing more than heating. Then you can relax and enjoy watching your little ones' excitement at new discoveries. You can take the time to guide them gently away from danger instead of upsetting everybody by yelling at them as you busily whip up some elaborate dish.

If the best part of camping for your family is the eating, it's easy to take along a few tablespoons of wine in a small bottle (stand it up when you pack it, wrap a hot-pot lifter or a dish towel around it and fit it in snugly to avoid breakage) to give some dish that extra-special touch. A few cans of your favorite seasonings (oregano, rosemary, etc.) take up very little space.

If you want, you can premix the seasonings you will need for different dishes. Put them in empty plastic pill bottles or small plastic bags, and take them to camp—properly labeled, of course—all ready to stir into the pot.

On page 132 you'll find suggestions for easy appetizers and a beverage you can premix before leaving home.

## Packing Food Supplies for Four-Wheel Travel

When you pack your food supplies, do it in boxes. Don't pile foods one on top of the other in deep boxes so that you have to dig through to find what you want. If you sort the different things more or less by height, you can put them in appropriate-sized containers and be able to see what you've got. If possible, choose boxes that are small enough to handle easily and that can be set on the benches of picnic tables. Then you should be able to work right out of the boxes without unpacking everything. Pack the things so they don't quite reach the upper edge of the box. Then, if you have several boxes, you can stack them on top of each other if necessary.

There are camp "pantries" and "kitchens" that are glorified boxes of one kind or another for storing kitchen equipment, cans and packages of food, spices, etc. But for an overnight or weekend trip you should be able to get by very nicely without anything of the sort, especially if you go to an improved campground where there is a picnic table with benches to spread things out on.

After you've had a bit of experience, you'll know what *you* need for your camping trip. You might, for instance, want to sew up a shoe-bag type of contraption with labeled pockets for different things you regularly take with you.

What you may find good to have along right from the first is some S hooks for hanging up pots and pans and other cooking equipment. You can buy them from a camping outfitter or cut lengths from wire coat hangers and bend each into an S shape. Tie knots about ten inches apart in a length of clothesline. Then when you get to camp, tie the line between two trees. The hooks go between the knots, the pots and pans, etc. go on the hooks.

## A Last Word on Planning Ahead

In your practice camping at home, work out a rough plan of who will do what. You can perfect your routine during the first few camping trips so KP (kitchen police) won't be an unpleasant chore for anyone.

One thing that will make everything a shade rosier is having a snack and a drink packed in a handy place so everyone can take the edge off any driving fatigue and hunger before setting up camp—maybe individual packages of nuts and dried fruit for the children, maybe a ready-mixed jar of orange juice and sherry with plenty of ice (see recipe page 132), or an ice-cold beer for the driver.

## Cooking in Camp

**The Cooking Fire:** We tell you on page 151 how to build a cooking fire from wood. Here we want to remind you never to cook over that fire while it's still flaming. Wait until it has burned down and nothing is left except gray-ash-covered hot red coals.

We tell you on page 99 how to start a charcoal fire using a gadget called an "Auto Fire." The same cooking instructions apply to charcoal cooking. Don't cook over them while they are flaming.

Four inches is the right distance to place food above a good hot bed of coals. But, unless your bed is good and deep, the fire will soon cool down, so you will have to have an adjustable grate that you can easily raise and lower to meet the need of the moment.

If you do not cook on an adjustable charcoal stove but on a grate spread over a bed of coals, you will have to find different sized rocks to accomplish this feat. We have sometimes carried along four red bricks when we thought there would not be any rocks available. Turned on their side they're one height; laid flat they're another.

If you are going to cook vegetables buried in the coals or resting on top of them, you will need more coals than for broiling a rare steak. Don't expect to cover a thin layer of coals completely with baking potatoes and have enough heat left over to brown and cook a steak resting on a grate above them.

Consider these things when building your fire.

Timing: Adding to the problem of fluctuating heat from the coals, the wind has a chilling effect. This can be partially eliminated if you do your cooking in a sheltered spot.

One of the biggest problems in timing you're likely to run into is in high country, where the altitude throws things out of kilter. Sea-level boiling temperature is 212° F., while at 5,280 feet (one mile) it's 201°. At 10,000 feet it drops to 194°, which means that anything that's steamed, baked or boiled will take longer to cook. Some things at a mile high take almost twice as long to cook as at sea level. And, since food takes longer to boil, you must watch the pot and replace the liquid as it steams away.

All of which means just one thing: Relax. Don't plan any tight schedules around your eating, and use times given in recipes merely as a rough guide. You'll get used to the uncertainties and make them part of a less tense scheme of living.

## Recipes

Following are a few suggestions and what we consider good recipes for camp use.

Remember this when figuring quantities: No one but you can know what will make a satisfying serving for the members of your family. And if the members of your family are normal human beings, their appetites will be sharpened by fresh air and exercise. So use the quantities given in our recipes only as rough guides.

### Granola for Breakfast

This is our recipe for a mixed breakfast cereal that is very satisfying, very nutritious (good for either car camping or backpacking) and is becoming increasingly popular. Make it at home and carry to camp with you ready to serve.

   3 tablespoons cooking oil (we use corn oil)
   3 cups of slow-cooking rolled oats (the kind we use says 10
       minutes on the box)
   4½ tablespoons roasted sesame seeds (buy at health-food
       store)
   4½ tablespoons wheat germ
   ½ cup pretoasted coconut (we use Baker's Coconut
       Crunchies)
   ¾ cup dry roasted peanuts, crushed
   1 cup seedless raisins (substitute other dried fruit,
       chopped)

Mix cooking oil thoroughly into rolled oats and spread them out in a shallow 12-inch-by-18-inch pan. Bake in a 250° F. oven 20–30 minutes or until they turn a rich golden color and taste cooked. Stir once or twice during cooking process and watch them closely after the first 15 minutes. Mix thoroughly with all other ingredients, and after mixture cools, store in a covered jar. Makes about 12 half-cup servings.

NOTE: You can eat granola any way you like it. Dan and our son like it with plain yogurt mixed with a little honey. Inez likes to eat it dry while sipping a cup of tea. Some people pour apple juice or milk (canned or fresh) over it. For a backpacking breakfast you can eat it dry or with reconstituted powdered milk or apple juice.

VARIATION: You can add to the protein content by adding

3 tablespoons or to taste of soya bean granules, which you can buy at health-food stores.

### Biscuits Baked in a Pot Instead of in the Oven

2 cups of biscuit mix
Water or milk according to directions

Place a metal pie or cake tin upside down in bottom of a large heavy pot (at least 5-quart). Even better than the pie or cake tin is a short-legged round wire rack covered with aluminum foil. (The idea is to form a shelf above the bottom of the pot.) Put cover on pot and preheat for about 5 minutes at medium heat.

Prepare biscuit mix according to package instructions and drop by spoonful onto tin or foil-covered rack in bottom of pot. There should be about 12 biscuits. Cover immediately and cook, turned to medium heat (or medium coals if cooking over campfire). Check biscuits for doneness 2 or 3 minutes before time given on package. When done, remove pot from fire and let stand, with lid a little ajar, to keep warm for up to 10 minutes while you finish cooking the rest of the meal.

### Brown Rice

Brown rice is more nutritious than white and, we find, much more satisfying, which makes it ideal for the camp meal. There's a trick to cooking it so it's not gummy and here it is:

1 cup of brown rice
3 cups of water
1 tablespoon cooking oil
Salt to taste

Bring water to boil in a heavy pot. Add cooking oil and salt, and slowly stir in rice. When water returns to a boil, stir rice *just once more,* reduce to a very low simmer and put lid on pot. Cook without removing lid or stirring for 40 minutes. Then carefully check, without stirring, to see if rice is soft. (If you don't use a heavy pot, you will have to check it sooner.) All the water should be absorbed when rice is done, which usually takes 45 minutes. More time and water are needed in high altitudes.

If you don't get brown rice right the first time, try again and adjust the time and rate of simmering, always remembering not to stir after reducing heat to a low simmer. It's well worth the trouble of learning to cook it right.

### Beef and Tomato Soup

(A One-Pot Meal Ideal for Carrying to Camp in Vacuum Jars)

1 pound round steak cut into bite-size pieces
1 28-ounce can peeled tomatoes
1 16-ounce can stewed tomatoes
1 large carrot, scraped and sliced crosswise
1 medium onion, chopped
1 stalk celery, chopped
2 cups water

The day before going to camp combine all ingredients in a large, heavy pot and bring to a boil. Turn down to a simmer, cover and cook, stirring occasionally, for 2½ hours. Chill and refrigerate overnight. The next morning bring to a boil, cover and simmer for at least 5 minutes, stirring frequently. Pour into vacuum jars (see page 108) that have been preheated with boiling water and immediately seal. Makes enough to just fill two 4-cup jars and, served with slabs of good-quality bread, will make a hearty meal for 4 to 6.

NOTE: This soup is even better made with chunks of oxtail, but you have to remove the meat from the bones before reheating to pour into jars.

### Ground Beef

"Hamburger" is the cheapest form of ground beef, chuck comes next, with ground round at the top of the price list. The fat these three types of meat contain is directly opposite to their price; ground round has the least, while hamburger has the most, which accounts for its excessive shrinkage. For cooking over the coals, we prefer a good-quality ground chuck. You may find ground round a little too dry.

### Our Favorite Ground Chuck Patties

1½ pounds ground chuck
1 6-ounce can tomato paste
¼ cup water
¾ cup prepared poultry stuffing crumbs
1 minced onion (about 4 ounces)

Thoroughly mix all ingredients and form into 6–8 patties about ¾ inch thick. Place in long-handled hinged wire grille and broil about 4 inches above hot gray burned-down cooking coals that are no longer flaming. Cook 6 to 10 minutes to a side or until just cooked through. Watch carefully and if outside is getting too brown, move farther from heat. Serves 4–6.

NOTE: You can make these patties thinner and serve on hamburger buns. You can also cook them in a frying pan on a camp stove.

HAMBURGERS AND CHAMPAGNE: If you are as unconventional as we are in our approach to camp dining, you can pack a bottle of champagne (wrap it and some fairly sturdy champagne glasses well in dish towels) in your cooler and take it along to serve with the beef patties. Until you've tried champagne and hamburgers, you haven't really lived!

### Ground Round with Green Pepper and Beans

#### (A One-Pot Meal)

1 pound ground round
2 tablespoons cooking oil
2 stalks celery, cut crosswise in ¼-inch slices
1 medium onion, sliced
1 green pepper, seeds removed and cut in slices ¼-inch thick
1 1-pound can baked beans
Salt and pepper to taste
Garlic powder to taste

Heat cooking oil in pot or large skillet. Add vegetables and sauté lightly. Turn down heat and cook until crisp tender.

Remove from pot. Add meat to pot and cook at low heat, stirring constantly, until all pink color disappears. Add beans and cooked vegetables, stir, cover and cook just until heated through, stirring frequently. Add salt and pepper and garlic powder to taste.

Serve with sliced tomatoes or tossed salad and bread or buns. Serves 4.

### Steak Over the Coals

Our favorite steak for broiling over the coals is choice boneless chuck, what our butcher calls "center cut." You can use any of the more expensive steaks if you prefer (except round, which is too dry for broiling), but we think that nothing has more flavor than chuck.

### Steak Seasoned with French Dressing

2 center cut chuck steaks, 1¼–1½ inches thick
2 tablespoons olive oil
2 tablespoons wine vinegar
Salt and pepper to taste
Garlic powder to taste

Combine olive oil, vinegar, salt and pepper and garlic powder and rub well into the steak. Place on grate or in long-handled hinged wire grille about 4 inches above burned-down cooking coals. Turn once and baste with the dressing as it cooks.

Approximate time to cook per side:
Rare: 6 to 9 minutes.
Medium: 10 minutes.
Well done: 12 to 15 (chuck steak may be a little tough if cooked very well done).

STEAK SEASONED WITH TAWNY PORT: Prepare as above but substitute tawny port wine for the French dressing.

BROILING STEAK OVER THE COALS WHILE PARTIALLY FROZEN: Be sure you have plenty of burned-down coals, because it will take from half again to twice as long to cook steak in a partially frozen state than if it's completely thawed. Start your steak cooking about 6 inches above the cooking coals instead of the usual 4 (frozen steak gets tough if you try to cook it too quickly and the outside may become more charred than you like before the inside is done), but move closer after the meat becomes completely pliant.

### Chicken Barbecued in Marinara Sauce

1 3- to 3½-pound young, tender chicken, cut into serving pieces
1 stalk of celery
2 carrots, scraped
1 large onion
1 teaspoon salt or to taste
1 15-ounce jar marinara sauce

The day before you go camping, put chicken in a pot, cover with cold water and add all remaining ingredients except marinara sauce. Bring to a boil, turn down to a simmer and continue cooking 15–25 minutes or just until chicken is done. Don't overcook.

Remove chicken from broth (you can reduce the broth to taste and serve it with the vegetables for dinner at home), drain and refrigerate overnight. Wrap and store in coldest part of camp cooler just before leaving.

At camp: Coat outside of each chicken piece with marinara sauce and place on grate (or in long-handled hinged grille) about 4 inches above burned-down cooking coals. Brown all sides of chicken, be sure it's heated through, and serve. Serves 4.

NOTE: If you want, you can freeze the reduced chicken broth with vegetables overnight in a wide-mouth plastic jar (leave a little expansion space), take to camp in your cooler, heat and serve the first night. You can even take along some premeasured matzoh meal and make hunger-satisfying matzoh balls (follow the recipe on the matzoh meal box) and cook in the soup. If the above recipe doesn't give you enough soup, take along a can of chicken soup, too, and combine the two.

### About Cooking Fish

Fish should never be overcooked. The instant the protein coagulates and the flesh loses its translucent appearance, the instant the flakes can be separated by probing gently with the tines of a fork, that's the instant the fish is ready to be eaten, and that takes very little time. As just a rough guide, you can estimate about 10 minutes per inch of thickness, but test it at half that time.

Try to plan your meal so that you can eat as soon as the fish is ready. It will taste *so* much better if it doesn't stand around.

### Fresh-Caught-Fish Chowder

#### (A One-Pot Meal)

1 to 1½ pounds of boneless fish fillets, any kind you happen
    to catch
¾ cup of water
Liquid from can of vegetables
2 10-ounce cans golden mushroom soup
1 16-ounce can mixed vegetables
1 16-ounce can sliced potatoes, drained
Salt and pepper and onion salt to taste

Put fish in pot, add water and liquid from vegetables (there should be about ⅔ cup), cover and bring to a simmer. Continue to cook just until the fish flakes separate easily when gently probed with tines of a fork (which sometimes will be no longer than it takes to bring the water to a simmer). Remove fish with a slotted spoon and set aside. Add mushroom soup to water in which fish was cooked and bring to a simmer, stirring constantly until smooth. Add mixed vegetables and sliced potatoes. Continue cooking at a low simmer, stirring frequently until vegetables are hot. Add salt (go easy because canned foods are fairly salty), pepper and onion salt to taste. Add fish, and as soon as it is heated through, serve. Serves 4.

NOTE: If you happen to have cream in your cooler, a little added to the chowder will give it a nice rich flavor. A teaspoon or so of sherry adds a nice touch, too.

If you have the ingredients and the time, this chowder is even better when made with fresh-cooked vegetables and potatoes.

## Pan Fish Fried in Batter

(From *The Complete Fish Cookbook,* by Dan and Inez Morris,
Bobbs-Merrill, 1972)

2 to 4 medium pan fish, freshwater or saltwater
1 egg, lightly beaten
¼ cup milk or canned milk diluted with water
½ cup toasted breadcrumbs, cracker crumbs or cornmeal
2 to 4 tablespoons olive or other cooking oil
Salt and pepper to taste
Lemon wedges

Combine egg and milk or canned milk, dip pan fish in the
mixture, then coat with crumbs or cornmeal and lay on a
clean, flat surface to dry 3–5 minutes. Heat oil in large skillet
to sizzling (but not smoking) hot. Add fish, fry until golden
brown on one side, turn and fry on second side or until
flesh flakes easily when gently probed with tines of fork.
Serve at once. Pass the salt, pepper and lemon wedges and
let individuals season to their own taste. Serves 2–4.

FISH FILLETS AND STEAKS FRIED IN BATTER: Fry fillets or
steaks from any fresh or saltwater fish you catch in the same
way as pan fish in preceding recipe. The more surface you
have to cover, the more you will have to increase quantities
of milk and crumbs.

## Brook Trout Poached in Wine

(From *The Complete Fish Cookbook,* by Dan and Inez Morris,
Bobbs-Merrill, 1972)

2 medium-sized brook trout or any other pan fish, freshwater or saltwater
1 good-sized pinch of dry mustard
2 tablespoons butter, margarine or hydrogenated vegetable oil
1 tablespoon soy sauce
1 teaspoon honey
¼ cup sherry wine
1 cup water
¾ teaspoon arrowroot (or substitute 1 tablespoon of flour)

In a large, heavy skillet, stir mustard into 1 tablespoon butter or margarine or vegetable oil until well blended. Add soy sauce, honey, sherry and water, still well and heat to boiling. Turn down to simmer and cook for 5 minutes. Add fish, cover and continue cooking for about another 5–10 minutes or until flesh separates easily into flakes when gently probed with the tines of a fork. Remove fish to a warm dish and cover to keep warm. Blend arrowroot with remaining tablespoon butter, margarine or vegetable oil and add to sauce. Cook, stirring constantly, until thickened. Pour over trout and serve. Serves 2.

BONED TROUT WITH NUTS AND RAISINS: Make Brook Trout Poached in Wine, bone the trout after cooking, reheat in sauce, add 2 handfuls each of nuts and raisins and serve over toast, potatoes or rice. This is a good recipe for making fish eaters (and avid fishermen) out of children.


### Charcoal-Broiled Camp Trout

(From *The Complete Fish Cookbook*, by Dan and Inez Morris, Bobbs-Merrill, 1972)

6 7- to 9-inch fresh-caught rainbow trout, dressed, or
    other freshwater or saltwater game fish
Salt and pepper to taste
Garlic powder to taste
2 tablespoons butter or margarine
Lemon wedges


Arrange trout in long-handled hinged grille and broil about 4 inches above burned-down cooking coals. Cook about 4 to 6 minutes to a side or until flesh flakes easily when gently probed with the tines of a fork. Serve at once and let each fisherman spread butter over his own hot fish and sprinkle to suit his own taste with salt, pepper, garlic powder and fresh-squeezed lemon juice. Serves 2–4.

CAMP TROUT BROILED WITH BARBECUE SAUCE: Cook as in foregoing recipe and baste with barbecue sauce of your choice.

### Foil-Baked Fish Chunks

2 fish chunks, about ¾ pound each
1 tomato, sliced
1 onion, sliced
2 tablespoons butter or margarine
4 tablespoons wine or water
Salt and pepper to taste
Garlic powder to taste

Place each fish chunk on a square of heavy-duty aluminum foil. Top each chunk with half the tomato, onion and butter or margarine, pour 2 tablespoons of wine or water over it, and season to taste with salt, pepper and garlic powder. Fold each square of foil into a package, double-folding all edges to seal, and lay on grate 4 inches above burned-down cooking coals. Turn packages once, cooking for a total of 15 to 20 minutes or until fish flakes easily when gently tested with tines of a fork. Serves 2.

NOTE: Pan fish can be cooked in the same way as in the foregoing recipe but test for doneness in about 10 minutes. Packages can be cooked directly on top of the coals instead of on the grate.

### Hot Dogs

We don't have to tell you how to cook them. We just want to remind you, if hot dogs will be the only thing your children eat at the meal you serve them (we're assuming your children like them as well as our children once did), you can make them more nutritious by taking along a can of sauerkraut to heat, then spoon over the frankfurters. Also buy the best-quality enriched buns you can find.

### Cabbage Boiled in Chicken Broth

Cabbage for four
2 13¾-ounce cans of chicken soup that needs no diluting
    or equivalent amount made from chicken or beef
    bouillon cubes or dehydrated broth
½ cup water

Wash cabbage and cut into serving-size wedges. Place in a large pot, add soup and water, cover and bring to a boil. Turn down to a low simmer and cook 20–30 minutes or until cabbage is done the way you like it. Serve the broth, leaving the cabbage covered, then serve the cabbage with the rest of your meal. Serves 4.

VARIATION: Add scraped carrots and/or peeled raw potatoes to the pot while cooking the cabbage.

### Corn on the Cob

Pull husks back from ears of corn and carefully remove all of silk. Wash corn in salted water and, without drying the ears, replace the husks and wrap ears in individual pieces of heavy-duty aluminum foil, double-folding to seal tightly. Bury the ears in burned-down cooking coals (or lay them on top of the coals) and cook for 6 to 8 minutes if they are young and tender, a little longer for older ears.

NOTE: You can cook the foil-wrapped ears of corn on the grate above burned-down cooking coals, but it will take 8 to 12 minutes. Turn them several times.

### Mixed Vegetables Baked in Coals

(From *The Complete Outdoor Cookbook*, by Dan and Inez Morris, Hawthorn Books, 1970)

You will need the following for each person to be served:
1 ¼-inch slice of large onion
1 square-foot piece of heavy-duty aluminum foil
1 small tomato, not more than 2½ inches in diameter, rubbed with 1 teaspoon butter or margarine
½ small zucchini, not more than 1½ inches in diameter, rubbed with 1 teaspoon butter or margarine
2 or 3 slices of celery, ¼–½ inch thick
Salt and pepper to taste.

Lay onion slice in center of aluminum foil. Arrange other vegetables on top of onion slice, season and wrap foil envelope-style, folding edges 3 times and sealing tightly. Bury packets in burned-down coals to cook. If they are not completely surrounded by hot coals, turn them once or twice during cooking process. The vegetables will be done in 15 to 25 minutes. Test one before opening other packets. Serve 1 packet to each person, using the foil as dish. If unopened and protected from the breeze, packets will stay warm for at least 10 minutes.

NOTE: Almost any assortment of small and/or sliced vegetables you want to put together and cook in the same manner as above will turn out well.

Packets can be laid on top of grate and cooked for 20 to 30 minutes. Turn several times.

### Foil-Baked Potatoes

Wash medium-large potatoes (about 8 ounces each), wrap individually in heavy-duty or double thickness of regular aluminum foil and seal with a double fold along all edges. Bury in a good bed of burned-down hot cooking coals or lay on top of them and bake until done. This will take anywhere from 40 to 60 minutes. Test by poking a fork right through foil covering. If you lay potatoes on top of coals, turn them several times while cooking.

FOR QUICKER-COOKING POTATOES: Our outdoorsman friend and Dan's co-author on several books, Norman Strung, taught us this method. Your potatoes will cook more quickly and consequently with less charring on the skin if you do this: Prick both sides of the potato skin with a fork and pour one teaspoon of water into each foil packet before sealing. Test for doneness at 30 minutes.

### French Salad Dressing

Olive oil
Cooking oil
Wine vinegar
Salt and pepper to taste
Garlic powder to taste

You can mix the above ingredients in any proportion you want, but we like it with a little more oil than vinegar.

Put it in a bottle that you can cork tightly, wrap a hot-pot lifter or some such thing around it to protect it and pack (upright) wherever there's space for it. It does not need refrigerating. Shake well and pour over tossed salad made of lettuce, onion and any other vegetables you happen to have at camp.

## Camp Desserts

Our favorite dessert when camping is fruit in season and cheese. Not only does it almost eliminate preparation and dishwashing, but it also helps fill in any nutritional gaps.

If you are going to want cake or cookies and you don't make your own, buy them at a store where you know they will be fresh and flavorsome. Don't count on campground stores for a good selection or a good price.

### Cherry Dumplings

    1 14-ounce jar canned cherries
    ½ cup prepared biscuit mix
    ¼ cup milk
    Canned milk or cream

Place cherries in saucepan and bring to a low boil. Add milk to biscuit mix, stir just until well mixed, then drop by teaspoonfuls on top of cherries. Cook 10 minutes without a cover, then cover and cook 10 minutes longer. Serve hot with canned milk or cream. Serves 3–4.

### For the Cocktail Hour

If you like to nibble and sip before your camp dinner, here are some simple suggestions that taste wonderful, are satisfying, refreshing, even nutritious, without adding much work.

Wash some celery and radishes the night before you leave home and take them along. Also take along a can of olives and some flat cans of smoked mussels or oysters. Then there's always those old standbys, cheese and the many delicious crackers now available.

### Orange Juice and Sherry

    4 glasses of cold orange juice
    ⅓ cup sherry
    Ice

Mix well, taste, add more sherry if you would prefer it that way and serve.

NOTE: You can premix the juice and sherry before you leave home.

# Chapter 5

---

# Things to Take Along
# That Will Keep
# the Children (and You)
# Occupied

---

It's quite possible that you won't need this chapter. It may be that, for the first time at least, the business of unpacking, packing, making and breaking camp, cooking, eating and discovering the outdoors will keep you busy. Or it may be that the sports and entertainment activities available at

the camp of your choice will fill up all the free time. Or you may have chosen an area where nearby sightseeing will keep you busy.

But, having raised two children (one quiet, one as active as if she had been constructed not of bones but of springs that made her jump with every move), we recommend taking along some insurance. What form it takes depends on your family and its interests and habits. Maybe it will rain part of the time. Maybe you'll don raingear and take an exhilarating walk. Maybe, on the other hand, you'll be confined to your car and tent.

If you all like to read and if you take along one interesting book per person, this can be fun. Or take books to read to small children. You can use storybooks as a point of departure for everyone making up stories.

If your family likes to draw pictures, take along pads (not loose paper), pencils and such things as felt pens for coloring (not boxes of watercolors or other messy things). Maybe coloring books and crayons.

Maybe traveling games with parts that peg into a board so they won't get lost. Puzzles. Playing cards for different types of games.

And you can find books of games at the library that include some for quiet times.

Although the number of toys each child is permitted to take should be limited, don't say no to a favorite small doll or maybe a few miniature dinosaurs that you know are an important part of your children's make-believe games.

If you are going to a camping area where you can pursue a specific hobby—nature identification, fishing, gathering and identifying seashells, rock hunting, panning for gold or whatever—be sure to make a list of the books and equipment you need and take those things with you.

See also page 16, Part I, Chapter 2 for additional suggestions.

# Chapter 6

# Lists

Once you have decided to go on a camping trip, you'll want to make up a list of the things to take. It's hard to sit down and just write a complete list without overlooking something. Many people keep their list in a handy place (such as beside a frequently used telephone) so that as they think of additional things they can write them down. We keep several lists, one for each category of things, fastened to the refrigerator door with little decorative magnets. That's one place we're sure to remember.

Once everything is written down, compile your list into neat form, whatever is best for you. Some arrange things alphabetically, others by category. Then as you pack each item check it off.

Don't throw your list away. Keep it to use next time and cross off any items you take along the first few times that you find are superfluous.

Following is a list of things that may be suitable for you. Use it as a departure point, changing, adding to or deleting from as necessary. *Add any appropriate items from lists in boat and canoe camping chapters. If you are going backpacking, see list on page 88.*

## Baby's Special Needs

Bottle liners and bottles
Car or other bed, blankets and possibly a bunting
Disposable diapers

Food and vitamins
Mosquito netting covers
Warm sleepers
Other

## Clothing

Bathing suit, beach robe (to double as bathrobe) and beach
    sandals
Boots
Changes of under and outer garments and socks
Gloves
Hat, cap, head scarf
Pajamas
Rainwear (rubbers and poncho)
Sweater or thick woolen shirt
Thermal underwear
Windbreaker

## Cooking and Eating Equipment

Aluminum foil
Camp cooler
Can opener (a good one) and beer can opener
Cooler and ice
Cooking utensils: pots, coffee pot, frying pan, pancake
    turner, cooking fork, slotted spoon, measuring and stirring
    spoons
Dish pan
Dish towels
Eating utensils: plates, cups, knives, forks and spoons
Food supplies made up from your own recipe checklist
Grate for cooking fire
Ice pick
Matches (old-fashioned kitchen) in waterproof case. If
    safety matches are used, be sure to take something to
    strike them on. For extra security, waterproof matches
    with paraffin or nail polish.

Paper napkins and towels
Plastic bags
Plastic tablecloth
Pot holders
Scouring pads
Seasonings such as salt, pepper, catsup, etc.
S hooks and clothesline to hang them on
Soap for dishes
Sponges
Stoves (charcoal and/or camp and fuel)
Tea, coffee, milk, juice, etc.
Vacuum jars
Water carriers

## Fun and Games

See "Things to Take Along to Keep the Children (and You)
Occupied" and make up a list that's appropriate for you.

## Miscellaneous

Binoculars
Camera and film
Chairs, folding
Fire extinguisher
Flashlights and extra batteries
Insect repellent
Lantern, fuel and mantles if needed
Lime for latrine
Needle and thread
Safety pins
Towels

## Shelter, Etc.

Blanket pins
Cots

Ground cloths for sleeping bags and tent
Mattresses (and pump for air mattresses)
Mosquito netting
Pillows and pillow cases
Sleeping bags or blankets, sheets or liners
Tarpaulins (including dining fly), ropes, poles, stakes (if
    to be used as a tent: clothesline, light line, clothespins)
Tents, poles, ropes, stakes plus at least 4 extra-long stakes

## Toilet and Health Articles

Brush and comb
Deodorant
First-aid kit (see page 62) and first-aid booklet
Shaving equipment
Soap
Toilet paper (even if you are going to a commercial camp-
    ground, take it along just in case)
Toilet seat covers
Toothbrush
Toothpaste
Towels
Washcloths

## Tools

Axe (or possibly a hammer for pounding)
Broom
Ice pick
Knife (pocket)
Repair kits for tent and air mattresses
Shovel
Saw (folding)

# PART III

# At Camp

# Chapter 1

---

# Choosing a Campsite

---

*When entering a forest or park area where you expect to camp, if there is a ranger or other official on duty, advise him where you will be and how long you expect to stay. He will be happy to answer any questions you may have and tell you of any regulations you should know about. (You should have found out before leaving home all about hunting and fishing licenses you might need.)*

Okay, you've gotten to where you want to go—and now to make camp for the next day or two. But where? And how? Here are the answers:

• First of all, do not pitch your tent, maneuver your tent trailer or park your pickup near the edge of a running stream or body of water. Far better that you move back at least 20 yards to a spot of high ground that will keep you well above the bugs and the mist, and so that water from a sudden shower will drain away from your tent rather than through it. It doesn't have to be the top of the highest hill, but it shouldn't be the side of a hill either.

If you're going to camp near a flatland lake, river or the seashore, the earth contours may be deceiving. So, if you can't tell high ground from low by looking, do this: Fill a cup half full of water and set it on the ground. The tilt of the water will tell you what's up and what's down. If there is no high ground, make camp 20 yards from shore.

• Although you're choosing high ground that's away from the water, don't get carried away and choose a spot that's too far away. You'll need water for cooking, etc. during your stay, and a bucket full of the stuff gets heavier the farther you carry it.

• Don't ever make camp in a gully, ravine, gulch, arroyo, etc., especially if you're on the desert. Dry as powder though they may be when you get there, one rainstorm and they can turn into pathways for raging torrents. They're called "flash floods" and you don't ever want to meet one head on.

• Also stay away from hollows. They may not be flash-flood channels, but they will fill up with enough rainwater to ruin your stay.

• Face your tent so that the opening is to the east and, if possible, so that trees are to your west. Reason: A lovely sunrise to waken you and the invigorating heat of the morning sun to start your day; shade in the afternoon to cool you during the hottest part of the day.

But stay well away from the tallest trees in the area. In an electric storm they are prime targets for lightning. The best trees to camp among from the standpoint of storm safety are those whose trunks are no more than six inches thick. Not only are they least lightning prone and not only will they bend with the wind, they also can serve as poles around which to tie your clothesline or whatever.

• Stay away from thick grass and thick brush. Not only are these bug areas, they are also definite fire hazards. But by all means, if such a spot is available, pitch your tent on low grass. It makes a wonderful mattress upon which to spread your bedroll. Clean, too.

• Stay away from steep hills and cliffs, particularly in springtime and autumn when frost movement can loosen rocks and send them tumbling down upon you. Freshly broken rocks strewn about are warning signs.

• If you're in an organized campground and you've been assigned a campsite that's beside a well-beaten path to toilets, swimming holes or other frequently used facilities, tell them you want another. The traffic can be terrific and guaranteed to go on both day and night, ruining your stay.

• If you are in snake country, which is mainly the desert, sleep up off the ground. Nighttime is a snake's time to prowl.

• If you camp by the sea or other tidal waters, make sure that your campsite is well above the high-tide mark.

# Chapter 2

# Making and Breaking Camp

Now you know where you are going to pitch your tent. But don't do it until you've swept the ground upon which it will stand. Clear away the twigs, pine cones, branches, stones, shells and whatever else will prevent you from having a smooth surface upon which to bed down. If you don't have a broom with you, find a dead branch and use it or part of it as a broom. Pick up with your hands anything that cannot be swept up.

Pick up your debris pile and deposit it in the nearest rubbish receptacle.

That's the first step in making camp. After that is done, do this:

- Spread your ground cloth and raise your tent, using extra-long stakes or extra tie-downs if you'll be camping in country where there are likely to be high winds.

- If on a beach or in desert sand, use extra-long stakes that are made for the purpose.

**Rain Ditches:** If your tent is not one that has mud- or splash-guard bottom edges and if you can't be sure that it won't rain during your stay, you'll have to dig a trench (called a "rain ditch" in camping circles) around the tent and a channel leading from the downhill side to carry the water away.

You'll have to, that is, if such ditching is permitted at the campground where you are staying. If not, you'll just have to put up with a little mud and dampness around the edge of your tent. Trenching is sometimes prohibited, and more often will be, because it is poor ecology to disturb the soil any more than is necessary.

Why is it poor ecology? Because it disturbs the roots of trees, destroys the sod and starts erosion. It also leaves a rough area of ground after you pack up your tent and leave.

However, if you are camping where such ditching is permitted or at least not prohibited, this is what you can do to rid yourself of rainwater while still helping to preserve the ecology:

• If on grass or weed bed, dig your ditch by taking up no more than a shovel-wide layer of earth just as you would sod on your lawn back home. Remove the sod carefully, roll it up or cut it into workable lengths, store it where the shade of a tree will protect it, and just as carefully replace it when breaking camp. Tamp it down gently, wet it down, and hope that the roots will take hold and the grass or whatever will grow again.

If your's cannot be a sod ditch, save the dirt and shovel it back in place when your stay in camp is over.

**Dining Fly:** If you think that your camp will not be complete without a dining fly, the place to erect it is a few feet in front of your tent so that you have, in effect, one great big living area. The tent is your bedroom, the dining fly is the roof over your combination open-air dining and living room. (Remember, though, that we told you to pitch your tent facing east.) So, if you are like us and want an unobstructed view of that marvelous sunrise while still snug in your bedroll, you'll want to erect your dining fly a bit to one side of your tent opening, but still in front of the tent, albeit obliquely.

**Cooking Area:** If you are going to cook over a portable stove, arrange your cooking area so that it will be a couple of feet to the east of your dining fly.

**Fireplace:** If you are going to have a campfire, build your fireplace (we tell you how in the next chapter) about 15 feet east of your dining fly, making sure that there are no overhanging branches or anything else that can catch fire above it.

If your campsite has a built-in fireplace, try to arrange your layout so that everything is still in that eastward-facing line—trees to the west for afternoon shade, then tent for morning sun, then dining fly and cooking area, then fireplace.

Why this emphasis on east other than for sun control?

The prevailing winds blow from the west in our hemisphere, and so the smoke and the odors and the bugs and everything else that travels with the wind will blow away from you.

**Toilet:** If you've brought a chemical toilet with you, all that has to be added is a shelter for privacy. Very simple. Somewhere not too far off, but not too close either, find four trees that stand in something of a square. Wrap a three- or four-foot width of tarpaulin, shower curtain, bed sheet or whatever around those four corners. Secure them so the shelter won't slide down, leave one end loose to serve as an entry flap and that's all there is to it.

If you are not camping in wooded area, fashion four stakes out of driftwood, dead branches, discarded lumber or whatever else you can find or have brought with you and they will do fine as your four corners.

The same shelter will do if you've brought along not a chemical but a safari toilet. There is one thing more that you must be sure to do: Remove the soiled plastic bag, tie it tightly and ask the camp, park or forest management where to dispose of it. If your camp has no disposal facility, we're so sorry but you'll just have to store those plastic bags out of sight and out of smell until it's time to go home again. Then take them with you and dispose of them at home.

**Latrine:** If you have neither chemical nor safari toilet, then you'll have to dig, man, dig, because the only recourse left to you is a woodsman's latrine. Find an isolated spot well away to north or south of camp (both under prevailing conditions should be out of path of the wind) and, most important, at least 125 feet from the water. And there dig a slit trench about three feet long, 12 to 16 inches wide, and at least one foot deep. Three feet is even better. Erect the same shelter around it that we told you about under the "Toilet" heading.

After each use, sprinkle first with a layer of dirt and then with some chlorinated lime. Leave the flap raised when not in use so as much air and sunlight as possible can get in.

We'll tell you what else you must do about latrines in the "Breaking Camp" section later on in this chapter.

**Water:** It well may be that you'll camp where no fresh water is available, and, take it from us, there are many such places: desert, seashore, some woodlands, and even some campgrounds do not have even a smidgin of water, not even tap water run in from a well or a municipal line. Therefore you'll have to pack your water with you in one of the containers that we listed earlier in this book (see page 109).

On the other hand, the only water available may be from a lake or stream instead of the usual tap you're accustomed to. We tell you on page 114 how to purify such water and make it usable.

**Dishwater and Its Disposal:** The time to heat water for doing the dishes and pots is when you start preparing the meal. It will take that long to get to the proper germ-killing temperature, especially over an open campfire.

The time to use that water, and then to dispose of it, is immediately after you've eaten.

And therein lies a problem. Namely, what to do with the dirty dishwater after you're done with it. The time has long since gone when you can just dump it on the ground because modern detergents contain destructive chemicals. Besides, it leaves a muddy mess for the next camper to contend with.

If you are in a supervised campground, find out from the manager what to do with the dishwater. In all likelihood the camp will have provided for its disposal.

If not, or if you are camping on private lands or in the wilderness where there are no such niceties as dishwater disposal sinks or pits, you'll have to dig your own. Since you'll be camping only a day or two, it need not be a big or deep one.

This is what to do:

• At an isolated spot, not too far from camp and downhill from any body of water (whether it's a large lake or trickling stream) or at least 125 feet away if that's impossible, dig a derby-shaped pit about 12 inches in diameter and 15 inches deep, taking care to remove the sod so that it can be replaced.

• Line the bottom of the pit with loose sand or gravel.

• Top that with a layer of pebbles.

• Top that with a layer of stones.

The pit is now ready to take your dirty dishwater. But be sure to dump only dishwater into it. Therefore food scraps and anything else of a more or less solid nature must first be removed.

When breaking camp be sure to replace the sod.

**Garbage Disposal:** Again, if you are in a supervised camp, this should be no problem. Some means of garbage disposal almost certainly will be available. If so, use it. If not, again, you'll have to dig a pit in which your garbage can be burned after each meal.

For overnight campers who wouldn't or shouldn't have much garbage to dispose of, the pit need not be overly large. About two feet square and two feet deep should do. And, of course, it should be located a good distance from camp and at least 125 feet from water. Use it after every meal, burning as much of your garbage as possible including not only all food scraps from your pots, pans and dishes, but also all used tin cans and aluminum foil.

When cool, flatten the cans with your heel, fold foil and put both cans and foil into a tote bag and on the way home discard them in a trash receptacle.

When breaking camp fill in the pit with dirt, stamp it down and replace the sod.

**Protecting Food from Four-Footed Marauders:** At home food that's left about attracts flies and other insects. In camp it also attracts such four-footed animals as bears, cats, squirrels and raccoons. So it behooves you to store everything possible in a tight-covered cooler, tight-covered pot or a tight-covered pretzel can.

Anything edible that for some reason will not fit into such containers—or if you're traveling light and have no such containers with you—should be hung from a tree branch that is at least seven feet from the ground. You needn't climb a tree to do that, however. Instead, place your raidable edibles in a food sack, tie the neck securely with several wraps of one end of a long length of line, toss the other end over the tree limb, hoist the sack high off the ground and wrap and tie the loose end of the line around and to the tree trunk.

Anytime you need something from the sack, unwrap the tree tie, lower the bag, remove the food and hoist the sack back into place again.

Some campgrounds where animals are a particular problem require that you store your food in covered containers inside your closed car. That way attractive odors are pretty effectively sealed away from snooping marauders.

## Breaking Camp

When leaving camp (outdoor folk call it "breaking camp") there is one fundamental rule to go by:

Leave your campsite better than when you found it.

• Fill in and resod all the pits and ditches you dug.

• Pick up every possible scrap of litter.

• Sweep and clean as you would your yard at home.

• If possible, stow everything that is to be disposed of in roadside receptacles in one container.

• Make sure that all fires are completely out, even those you built yesterday. The only foolproof way to tell is by placing your hand upon the ashes. If there's heat, there's fire.

So much for policing the area.

As for all the gear that you brought with you and are going to take home with you, remember this campers' rule: The end of one trip is the beginning of the next. In other words stow everything possible as if you were preparing to leave home for camp. The way you break camp will determine how easy it will be to make the next one.

Roll your sleeping bags tightly so they stow easily. Smooth your tent out and fold it firmly; keep poles, pegs and tarps together in another package. As you sift through and straighten your belongings, make notes about needed items: a tear in the tent that needs patching, a peg that needs replacing.

# Chapter 3

# The Campfire and the Cooking Fire

In many areas, it's necessary to obtain a fire permit before building a fire of any kind, so check into it if possible before leaving home.

When you build your campfire, you want to give consideration to two things: You don't want to set the woods on fire and you want to do the least possible damage to any sod.

The best way to accomplish both these things at once is to build the fire on sand or rock. Since this isn't always possible, we'll include instructions telling you how to build it on soil if you must.

Avoid building a fire on humus, which is like punk and in which fire can travel underground to pop up quite a distance away. If there is a ranger or other knowledgeable park or forest official available, ask his advice about where and how to build your fire in order to avoid this serious hazard in the particular area where you are camping. Never build it in dry grass or on the roots of a tree or against a tree, log or a stump or near a bush or under overhanging branches. And never build your fire any bigger than is absolutely necessary.

Clear a spot at least ten feet in diameter of all flammable material. Now you are ready to construct your campfire.

There are at least a dozen ways that we can think of to build a campfire, all of them good, but the one that we think is best for all-around camp use is what outdoorsmen call the "keyhole lay."

The fireplace looks just as you'd expect, like a keyhole, and it is very simple to shape. If building it on rock, collect stones and make a wall that will be at least six inches high and arrange them to form two connecting circles, one large, one small. If building your fireplace on sand or soil, collect stones that are about four inches high and arrange in the same way, but also dig out inside the circles to about a three-inch depth. When doing so, carefully preserve any sod and put it in the shade for safekeeping. When you leave, turn under the bed of ashes with a spade or shovel, return the sod, press it down gently and water it. You don't need to bother with the stones in the second method we describe if they aren't easily available. Just dig your hole a little deeper and build the sides up with dirt. The idea is to build a fireplace of the right depth so that your cooking grate will rest about four inches above the top of a bed of burned-down coals. If you can do this so that the height of the grate above the coals will be adjustable, so much the better.

Don't use slate or shale rock for fire building, as the heat will crack it. Porous rocks filled with water can be a hazard, because they may explode when hot.

Build a wood fire in the large circle of your fireplace for warmth and for sitting around. Rake hot coals from this fire into the small circle for cooking. Spread a wire grate over the small circle of rocks and that's the top of your stove.

Before you can build your fire you have to collect wood.

**Collecting Campfire Wood:** First of all, the most visible source of supply is absolutely out. A growing tree, we mean, and for several reasons: It's tough to cut; it will take too long to burn; when it does, if it does, it will give off too much smoke; and we have to start conserving our green-growing things if mankind is to survive, because they make oxygen, the very air we breathe. So look for other sources of supply:

• Dead trees that are still standing, preferably saplings.
• Hangers, meaning a dead sapling that has started to fall but got hung up on some foliage.
• Tree stumps.
• Tree stubs, meaning a standing dead tree whose top long ago fell away.
• Logs, meaning heavy limbs, trunks and tops of dead trees that lie on the ground.

• On a beach or a riverbank there is driftwood.

You'll need three sizes of wood, in this order: tinder, kindling, firewood.

The tinder can be only a handful of anything that will catch fire swiftly and then will burn quick and hot—dry leaves, pine needles, pine cones, small twigs, bark (birch is best), bits of wood splinters from stubs or stumps, even a loose wad of paper.

A bit larger than tinder is the kindling, which goes on a campfire next. It can be small, dry branches, or shavings whittled with a small knife from any dry piece of wood. Woodsmen swear by "fuzz sticks," which are nothing more than shavings that never quite make it to the ground. To make one all you need is a 12- to 18-inch-long core of about one-inch dry wood. Notch shavings into it from end to end but don't quite sever them; they'll roughly resemble a porcupine's quills. That's a fuzz stick.

Finally comes firewood, the stuff that you warm yourself with, the stuff that makes fine cooking coals. Which means lengths of wood no more than two or three inches in diameter.

It can be softwood or hardwood, the only difference being that you use more soft than hard because it burns more quickly. You should, however, try to avoid resinous woods, because they give off sparks. However, a grate laid across the fire will help dissipate the sparks before they can do damage. The best rule to go by is: Be prepared. Keep a bucket of water and a shovel standing by in case an emergency develops.

**Your Cooking Fire:** Lay a long, fat length of firewood in the large end of the keyhole. Against it, about amidships, loosely pile tinder. Lean kindling, including the fuzz stick with its porcupine ends pointing down around the tinder and against the base log. The result should look like the frame for half a tepee. Stand with your back to the wind, strike a match and set the flame to the tinder.

As the flames take hold and the wood burns down, add more to the fire and rake the coals into the smaller end of the keyhole. Set your grate above them across the top of the circle of stones, and you're ready to cook.

**Cooking on a Sand Beach:** You cook on the beach, any

sand beach, just as you would cook anywhere else, except that the keyhole fireplace will be easier to construct, because all you need do is scoop out a hole with your hands and build up the sides with sand instead of stones.

To make a slit trench fireplace in the sand, dig a hole 6 to 8 inches deep (depending on depth of coal bed you will need), 12 inches wide and 30 inches long. Slope the sides. Build the fire in the center of the trench and straddle it with a wire grate about 18 to 24 inches long. Thus you'll be able to feed it fresh wood from either end without disturbing any pots or pans sitting on the grate.

You may find it easier to cook in sand if you line your firehole and its edges with aluminum foil.

## Permanent Fireplaces

Many improved campgrounds, whether public or private, have permanent fireplaces built into every campsite. This is fine; in fact it might be all to your favor, except for one thing: Many of these fixed fireplaces have built into them a grate on which the foods that you cook must lie. This too is fine, except for one more thing: Those grates should be no more than four or at the most five inches above the firebed if the food is to be cooked properly, and therefore at its tastiest best. However, far too many of these campground grates have obviously been installed by craftsmen who know far more about brick and stone masonry than they do about cooking. Result: They position the grates much too far above the firebeds, sometimes as much as 10 and 15 inches above.

So, what to do about it? Line the firebeds of such fireplaces with bricks and stones until there will be no more than four or five inches between the bed of coals and the grate.

## Putting Out a Campfire

You need two things in order to put out a campfire properly, whether burning wood or charcoal: water and a stick.

Pour water over the embers, lots of it, and stir them steadily with the stick while so doing. Eventually the water will drown the sparks. The stirring will ensure that every spark is saturated and thoroughly extinguished.

# Chapter 4

# Play It Safe
# and Have Fun

Throughout this book we've pointed out how to buy and use equipment in the safest way. At the end of Part I we cautioned beginners against going camping for the first few times in wilderness country unless accompanied by experienced campers, and we gave you some specific information about how to contact such people.

Here, now, we will cover just a few things we have not yet touched on that you will encounter once you get to camp.

*The greatest peril that you will run into in camp will not be snakes and wild animals, but your neighbor's pet dogs and automotive vehicles!*

In order to get the most from your stay at camp, ask the management for information about the area and what its particular attractions are that you may not already know about. Ask what specific hazards there are, particularly in regard to small children and what the regulations are that you should observe, particularly in regard to fire building.

One of the first things you should do is instruct your children where they can and where they cannot go on their own, giving special attention to water. Take them on a tour during the daylight hours, familiarizing them with the route to the bathroom or privy. Point out the danger from cars whose drivers may be searching for campsites and not watching out for playing children.

You should stay away from wild animals, enjoying their beauty from a distance. If they make a nuisance of themselves around your campsite, a flashlight or beating on a pan or yelling will probably scare them away. Don't pick up any baby animals thinking they are abandoned. Mama is probably nearby watching, and she may show her possessiveness in an unpleasant way.

Snakes are not anxious to be around strangers. But if you startle or frighten them, they may attack in self-defense. Our daughter, who lives on the New Mexico desert, has found that if she meets a snake, all she has to do is stand perfectly still, and it will go about its business without bothering her.

Turn boards or rocks over carefully, and never stick your hand into a hole. Since your shoe might be a hole to a spider, shake it out before putting it on. And keep your tent door zipped shut when you are not using the tent.

Hornets, wasps and bees sometimes can be pests when you are eating fruit or other sweet things. You may be able to divert them from your table by setting out a saucer of honey or syrup or watermelon rinds a comfortable distance away.

Poison oak and poison ivy have clusters of three shiny leaflets somewhat resembling oak leaves. Sometimes they have white berries. Poison sumac is an eastern shrub that has 7 to 13 gray-green leaflets, and it too sometimes has white berries. If possible, find out if these or any other troublesome plants grow around camp. If they do, point them out to your children so they can learn to avoid them.

Washing with brown soap immediately after coming in contact with one of these plants may prevent getting an unpleasant, itchy rash. If your dog is camping with you, keep him out of these plants, too, because you can pick up the poison by touching his fur if he has come in contact with them.

The kind of camp you start out your camping experience in will probably have places where you can go on walks in perfect safety, if not alone, then with a guided group. But you will always need to use common sense.

Never start out on even just a little walk away from the campground without telling someone where you are going. Once you get out of sight of camp, it's much easier to lose your sense of direction than you may think. So stay on clearly marked trails. If you come to a fork in the trail, don't go any farther unless the trail back to camp is clearly marked.

The National Safety Council sums hiking up with these succinct words: "Stay on the trails, stay with a group, stay put if lost."

And we can sum up this chapter just as succinctly: Use common sense in all things that you do while camping and you'll have an unforgettably good time.

# PART IV

# Boat and Canoe Camping

# Chapter 1

## Boat Camping

On Long Island's South Shore there are hundreds of square miles of spoiled wetlands—marshes that never again will know the call of the wild. They were made so by the needs of man and the greeds of some men who pocketed their loot and called what they have done and are doing "progress."

But within that vast destruction that man has wrought upon nature there still remain many square miles of reasonably wild wetlands wilderness where the fish come to spawn and raise their young; where gulls, terns, plover and long-legged cranes come to feed; where ducks and geese, snow owls, coots, kingfishers, and even once in a while an eagle and many more come to rest their wings on long flights north and south and back again. Long Island's South Shore wetlands are a vital part of the Atlantic flyway and will so remain for as long as man's growing awareness of ecology is strong enough to overcome his greed. It is here that life begins; it is here that life well might end.

And it is here that are located our favorite one-day outing and overnight campgrounds—Long Island's South Shore wetlands, on the western fringes of them to be exact, recognizable by the long ribbons of concrete highways, all of them leading to one place: Jones Beach, the summertime oceanfront playground supreme for New York City cliff dwellers and their suburban neighbors by the millions. Take any Saturday and Sunday in the summer, take them if you dare, and watch the cars inching along those concrete ribbons. Bumper to bumper. Overheating. Steaming. Crawling to Jones Beach and a few precious inches of sand.

Amid all this is our favorite overnight campsite—rather we should say campsites, because there are so many of them to choose from, unspoiled, untouched, unreachable by car, reachable only by boat. That is where we love to camp. We can see the cars. We can see the spires of Manhattan. We can see the jets flying into and out of John F. Kennedy Airport. But none of the occupants of any of them notice us, because we are so completely isolated, so completely removed from man.

All this we have less than ten miles from our house. But, more importantly, less than 35 miles from New York City. All this we have now, because we own a boat. But all this we also had before, because then we simply rented a boat.

All this you may be able to have, too. There are sites reachable only by water ideally suited for camping in many places in America. We know, because we have seen them in our cross-country auto-camping trips. In 1970 on one such trip, we visited for several days with our good friends Garner and Kay Byars in Corinth, Mississippi, and we fished the TVA's Pickwick Lake by johnboat, and we cruised the Tennessee River by houseboat where the states of Mississippi, Tennessee and Alabama meet. It seemed that everywhere we looked on shore there were isolated glens perfect for pitching a tent or spreading a sleeping bag and bedding down for a night or two.

The story was the same on a trip that took us to Mark Twain's hometown of Hannibal, Missouri. We enjoyed a sidewheeler riverboat ride on the Mississippi. True, we saw many factories and lots of pollution—enough to make Tom Sawyer and Huckleberry Finn cry—but we also saw many ideal campsites on shore that are relatively untouched by man.

And so the story is the same everywhere in the United States and Canada where there is navigable water. Explore the shores, explore the islands, and you'll easily find by-boat-only campsites. All of them are easily accessible with the kick of an outboard, the stroke of an oar or a paddle, the billowing of a sail. None of them is accessible either by foot or by automotive vehicle.

The best way, we think, of boat camping is to own an outboard motorboat, hop into it and go. If you've never boat camped before, one day take a cruise specifically to seek out likely campsites. You'll be amazed at how many spots you discover. We said, for example, that our favorite locale is about ten miles from home, but there are many others that we pass along the way, some of them as close as a half-mile from home.

Generally speaking, much of the land bordering on major waterways is owned by municipal, county, state or federal government, and you usually camp there for a night or two.

Then again, it might be privately owned. The best way to tell is by the proximity of homes, factories or other man-made structures. If so, shun them if for no other reason than that by cruising a bit longer you'll probably soon come to a place that's been unspoiled by man. Mark it in your memory and make that your destination next weekend for your first boat-camping holiday.

If you decide you'd like to camp on someone's private property, be sure to ask permission.

If your favorite spot has been chosen by other boat campers or picnickers for use on Saturday and Sunday and it's within an hour's travel from home, don't let a job stop you from an overnight camp-out during the middle of the week. Maybe you have teenage kids who can help your wife set up camp during the day, and they can pick you up after work and whisk you out there *before dark.* Maybe you boat with a family of friends, and the kids and the gals can get camp set up during the day with one boat, and you and the other man can join them in the second boat as soon as you're through work. So what if you have to get up at the crack of dawn the next morning in order to be on time for work? Everyone should have the thrilling experience of at least one waterside camp sunrise in his lifetime. There is nothing quite like it.

There are many types of boats that are ideal for camping, and many ways of getting them to water. Let's look at them one at a time.

## 16- to 18-Foot Outboard Motorboats

Outboards within this footage range are most seaworthy and therefore best for people who live on the East Coast, West Coast, Gulf Coast, Great Lakes and major rivers such as the Mississippi. The 16-footer is good for families of no more than four, the 18-footers for families up to six and the 17-footers for the families in-between.

They should be made of fiberglass, as they're much easier to maintain than wood, and, besides, good wooden boats are becoming increasingly harder to find. The one big disadvantage of fiberglass: It won't float. And so synthetic materials ("flotation" is the all-encompassing word for such materials) must be built into boats made of such material to keep them from sinking. Not only, however, should flotation be sandwiched within the bottom, but also a goodly amount of it should be high up to keep the boat from turning bottom side up if it should fill with water.

For smoothest riding, maximum seaworthiness and ease of operation in shallow water—shallow water being where you will camp—a triple-entry hull is the shape we think is best. The trade calls such shapes by several names, chief among them "gull wing" and "cathedral," because in appearance that is what their undersides most resemble: a gull on the wing, a cathedral with its spires cutting into the sky.

But whatever they're called, this is the ideal shape for use in waters where stability counts, particularly on days when the seas are rough. Triple-entry hulls take more of a beating, ride easier and more smoothly, have less bounce, pound least and take turns without undue list.

Some outboards of these lengths, you'll find when shopping around or visiting boat shows, have cabins built into them. Our advice to you: Don't buy one. Cabins will rise higher than any other point on the boat, and in bad weather the wind may hit the cabin like a kite and cause you no end of trouble.

If you want a cabin boat, buy either a stern drive or an inboard cruiser, both of which we'll touch upon later.

Although they can be trailered behind a car, outboards of such length are best left in the water from season's start to season's end, which is another way of saying that if you do

not have a mooring berth, you'll have to rent a slip at a marina or an anchorage at a boat basin as near as possible to where you live.

Boats of this size should be powered by outboard motors of from about 35 to about 85 horsepower, depending upon the size of the boat and whether or not you also plan to use it for water-skiing. Manufacturers are now glutting the market with motors that range upward of 100 horsepower and are trying to brainwash the public into buying and using them. We can think of no situation that would call for so much power on so small a boat. We can think of many ways in which so much power could cause a lot of trouble, perhaps pain, perhaps death.

So our advice to you is worth repeating: Make 85 horse-

power your limit and use that large a motor only if you're going to tow water-skiers behind an 18-foot boat.

A fact worth noting right here: A 50-horsepower motor will very nicely, very smoothly, very pleasantly deliver an 18-foot boat and its cargo of people to any campsite you ever set out for. Very safely.

The package price of a 16- to 18-foot boat and a 35- to 85-horsepower outboard motor: $2,000 to $4,000, depending upon the size of each, where, when and from whom you buy.

## 13- to 15-Foot Outboard Motorboats

Usually called "runabouts," these are the lengths that are best suited for families of four or fewer who live, camp, cruise and fish in lake and calm inland water country. Some manufacturers make outboards of these sizes with triple-entry hulls, but the conventional V shape in which wooden boats are made are almost the general rule. The V is the shape of the front half of the bottom and the flattening out in the rear end gives you a smooth-riding planing surface.

Such hulls may also be called "modified V" or "semi-V," but more important than the name, what does "planing surface" mean? Answer: While standing idle or cruising at low speed the boat will lie low and flat in the water; give it full throttle and first the bow and then the stern will lift out of the water, and suddenly, smoothly, the boat once again will level off and you will find yourself skimming the surface. That's what the boatmen call "planing."

Ease back about one-third on the throttle and you'll find yourself cruising along at an exhilarating speed but with minimal use of fuel.

Runabouts are fine for towing behind a car, although there's no law against berthing them during the boating season in a marina or boat basin. Since they trailer nicely, the runabout is just about the perfect outboard for the weekend camper who must travel by automotive vehicle to his favorite reachable-only-by-road campground. But then, provided it has nearby launching facilities, there is no reason he must camp there.

All he need do is stow gear and passengers into his boat, start the motor and cruise to an offshore island or opposite shore glen and camp there until it's time to head for home again.

Runabouts within the 13- to 15-foot class are adequately propelled by motors that range from 15 to 40 horsepower. Again the determining factors in matching motor to boat is the length of the latter and whether or not you'll be doing any water-skiing.

The price: anywhere from about $700 to about $2,000.

**Facilities:** The same sleeping, cooking and toilet gear that you'd have to take with you for any other weekend camping trip is the gear that you will have to take with you on an outboard motorboat camping trip. Such boats do not come equipped with such facilities, and if by the time this book is published there should be such a boat on the market, our advice to you is this: Don't, we repeat, don't buy it.

An outboard is meant to be an open-cockpit boat, the cockpit being the uncluttered space between windshield and transom, which is the boat's rear wall. Anything added to the cockpit, other than the seats that you'll already find there, can only get in your way, hamper your movements, perhaps cause fire if the addition happens to be a stove, and almost certainly cause inconvenience, if not trouble if the weather should suddenly kick up.

However, there is one bit of camping gear that has become available for the larger outboard boats in the past year or so that you may well want to consider having. It is, of all things, a tent. Only the makers don't call it a "tent." Instead, they call it a "camper top," and you can have one added to your boat simply by so stating at time of purchase and paying the price. Or, if the particular boat that you prefer does not have such an optional piece of equipment available, there is nothing to prevent you from having a tent-maker make one for you. The man who sells you the boat will be able to steer you to one.

The regular canvas cover that comes with most outboards connects to the hull with snap links and fits snugly to the lines of the hull. So does the camper cover, up to the hooking to the snap links, that is. But then comes the difference: Instead of clinging to the lines of the hull, it opens up to a tent as large as the boat's cockpit and tall enough to permit you to stand upright, or at the most with a slight stoop. It all depends on how tall you are.

Such a boat tent makes it unnecessary for you to sleep on *terra firma,* although everything else that goes with camping needs must be done there. Well, practically everything else. You'll have to cook on land, but there is no law against washing up aboard the boat if the spirit so moves you and you're willing to use cold water. Also there's no law against your bringing along a cooler full of enough cold food to last you for an overnight trip, plus a thermos of hot coffee for breakfast.

As for beds, most of today's outboards have two sets of back-to-back seats that open up into bunks which are standard equipment. If not, you can opt for them. So automatically you have beds for two of you. If there are more in your camping party, at least one person (perhaps two if small enough) can sleep on a foam or air mattress stretched between the two bunks. Anyone else will have to sleep on shore.

## Cartop Boats

Many is the man who loads his family and gear into camper, auto or station wagon and heads up the high road to a rutted turnoff that leads to a high-country lake or a lazy back-country river, and when he gets to his favorite off-the-beaten-path campsite, pulls to a halt and beds down for a delightful stay. Or rather, it could be delightful except that there are other people who know that spot, too, and maybe they'll also be there. And maybe, even if they're not, their left-behind debris will be.

Many is the camper who has the means of overcoming such a situation simply because he has a boat on the top of his automotive vehicle—called a "cartop boat"—which he intends to use only for fishing or nautical meandering.

Never does he dream, poor fellow, that that boat is his vehicle for escape from the evils of civilization. All he has to do is load up and take off for an unspoiled-by-man campsite on an island or on the opposite shore, downriver or upriver—any place that can't be reached by automotive vehicle, by foot or on horseback.

If you want to include yourself among the campers who already have discovered this approach to solitude, there are two boats for you to choose from. One is the johnboat, the other is the semi-V that's made for cartopping. They're from 10 to 12 feet in length, weigh no more than 150 pounds, and one healthy adult male can wrestle one atop a car and off again without undue strain.

Built like a midget-sized barge, the johnboat is a good craft to have if you plan to explore slow to moderately fast rivers, small lakes and protected inland waters. But stay away from them if you plan to do your boating in waters that develop much of a chop or where heavy weather is a threat. At the least, they're guaranteed to put lots of spray in your lap, at the worst they could flip you into the drink. Nor, despite their flat-bottom design, will they carry too much of a load.

On the positive side, they're cheap and they make ideal platforms for casting and fighting a fish.

The only difference between the cartopper semi-V and larger outboard motorboats is their size, and so the semi-V is the craft to have in any water, salt or fresh, where the elements can turn against you.

Cartoppers are made of plywood, aluminum, plastic, Styrofoam, fiberglass, and a combination of wood and canvas. Aluminum is the best bet, we think, for a cartopper because of its light weight and strength and the years of dependable service that it will give you even in saltwater. For saltwater use they should be made of a long-lasting marine aluminum. Plastic and Styrofoam are fast gaining in popularity, but they're on the bottom of the hull-material list as far as we're concerned, because riding in one of them is like riding in a bubble and, we're afraid, no more dependable.

Cartoppers will accommodate motors up to 12 horsepower, but we'd advise against anything larger than 5 for several reasons: The small motor will move you almost as fast, is perfect for trolling, will not take up so much room in your car trunk, is lighter to carry and easier to mount and dismount, and costs less.

Cartop boats, because of their size, won't carry much of a load. But no matter how large your family, water-going safety need not bother you. Just shuttle the people one at a time across to your opposite-shore campsite—or at most, two at a time. It's as simple as that.

A cartop boat with motor should cost somewhere between $200 to $600.

Canoes can also be carried atop your car, but since they are so very much a vehicle for camping, we'll give them a section all their own later on.

## Stern-Drive Boats

Also known as inboard-outboard motorboats, they're the kind of power to have for any craft that is from 18 to 24 feet in length. Our advice to you: 18 feet or below, stick to outboard power; above 24 feet, move up to inboard power.

Or another way of saying it: A stern-drive boat is the perfect in-betweener. They're so called because the motor is located inside the hull, while the drive unit is located outside the back ("transom" is the boatman's word for rear end).

Because manufacturers will make anything that the public will buy, stern-drive boats may or may not come complete with cabin and all the appurtenances needed for comfy-cozy onboard living. However, we don't think any boat of less than 21 feet should be so outfitted, and we suggest that, if you're in the market for a cabin boat, you confine your search to upwards of that figure.

Stern-drive boats are made mainly of fiberglass, and one will cost anywhere from $5,000 to upwards of $10,000. It all depends upon length, horsepower and how you have it outfitted.

Use the cabinless stern-drive boat of less than 21 feet as you would an outboard for weekend boat camping. With a cabin you can sleep in them on the water just as you would a fully equipped recvee on land. Pull out of the boating channel, drop anchor and bed down for the night. The facilities for cooking, etc. are not much different than those at home, so we'll say no more about them.

Just as the land recvee has its campgrounds where it can pull in and stay for the night, so too are there marinas where boats with living quarters can pull in and stay for the night. Since this, strictly speaking, is not camping, we'll also say no more about that here.

## Inboard Boats

Now we're getting up into the big-boat, big-money class. Any power craft beyond 24 feet should have its motor drive unit positioned inside the hull—which means that the *Queen Elizabeth* is an inboard, as is every ship in the Navy.

And if your name is Onassis you can buy them that big. They come in all sizes, shapes and dimensions; they have all the conveniences of home; they are not meant to be run in close to the beach; you don't need one or want one to picnic or camp out.

But if you own one and yet have a hankering for onshore camping, carry a dinghy aboard, use it as you would a cartop boat for getting to your campsite from your anchorage, and have fun.

*There is one thing wrong with power boats that we did not mention before, because as this is being written the machine-engine industry—or at least some segments of this industry is working to correct it—and that is pollution. All outboard engines built prior to about 1971 spilled gas and oil into the water, but since then at least one major manufacturer has come out with an engine that is claimed to be pollution-free. And we hope that by the time you read this all outboard manufacturers will have followed suit.*

*However, if you believe as we do in the vital necessity of conservation of our environment and you can't obtain a pollution-free engine, there are ways that you can still become a boat-camping enthusiast, namely by sailing, rowing or canoeing to your destination.*

## Sailboats

The one sailboat that we think is ideal for camping is the centerboard, so called because its keel (or centerboard) can be raised or lowered in a special well amidships. Thus simply by lifting the centerboard until, if necessary, it is practically flush with the bottom of the hull, the craft can be sailed into extremely shallow water.

Centerboarders range in size from 8-foot catboats to heavy-weather sloops 30 feet or longer. Any one of them up to about 18 feet is just about the perfect boat for nautical folk who want a weekend of camping and sailing without any of the evils of power craft that sailing buffs call "stink pots."

It makes no difference where you do your sailing, fresh water or saltwater, choppy or glassy. Stick to a centerboarder, and if you've mastered all the intricacies of sailing and nautical safety that you should, you'll have a grand time.

A centerboarder large enough to carry three or four people, meaning 12 feet on up to about 16 feet, should cost somewhere between $1,000 and $2,500.

Much smaller, much lighter and much less seaworthy than the centerboarders are the craft that somewhat resemble surfboards with sail attached. They're known as "sunfish" and "sailfish," and they are loads of fun on warm days in a light to moderate wind on small lakes and bays. They're easy to carry atop your car, they cost from about $350 on up, and they're okay for ferrying people and supplies back and forth from launch site to offshore campsite. They're also a good boat upon which to learn the rudiments of sailing. But don't expect to use them for daylong cruising.

And be prepared to take a dunking, because sunfish and sailfish are tippy. In other words, wear life jackets or stay in wade-ashore waters.

Above 24 feet there is also a sailing craft that has what is known as a "fixed keel." This is the sailing man's equivalent of the inboard power cruiser, and since they're ideal for long cruising rather than for weekend camping, we'll say no more about them.

## Collapsible Boats

A substitute for the cartop boats that we've talked about, both power and sail, are those that are carried not on the roof but in the auto trunk or station-wagon bed—collapsible craft that can be deflated or broken down into a small package. There are two major kinds: folding boats and rubber rafts.

Folding boats are just what the name implies. Their hull is canvas on rubberized cloth stretched over a wooden frame that is hinged, pinned and clasped so that they fold up like a deck chair for hauling or storage. They start at about $150 and they come in two hull styles: a square transom design that can be used with a small outboard motor, and a double-ended kayak. They're responsive to oars and paddles and, pushed along by a three- to five-horsepower motor, can manage up to eight knots (or, as a landlubber would say, about nine miles an hour). But they're fragile craft whose light weight makes them hard to handle in a wind.

They're okay, though, for funning and for ferrying people and supplies to offshore campsites when both the water and the wind are lying down nice and easy.

Rubber rafts can be bought for about $50 for a one-man job and can go as high as $1,500 for the great balloonlike boats used on commercial float trips down wild rivers.

They came into being during World War II as a space-saving lifeboat for flyers shot down or forced down at sea. Today, because they are virtually untippable, they are a good vehicle for boatless families to have for camping.

All rubber rafts have at least two air compartments; thus it will take a freak accident to sink one, and thanks to their beachball nature, they will bounce off solid objects such as rocks and logs.

Don't think of them as family boats, though, because that a rubber raft will never be. When it comes to propulsion, for example, rowing one is like paddling around in an inner tube, and using an outboard motor on those which come with motor mounts might mean less work but you won't go much faster.

## Boat Rental

If you don't already own a boat and if you have no intention of ever buying one, don't let that prevent you from going boat camping next weekend or the weekend after that, because you can rent just about any craft that we've described. Just consult the yellow pages of the telephone book and look under "Boats—Rental & Charter."

What it will cost you to rent a boat for a weekend is dependent on several factors, chief among them the kind and size of boat you have your eye on and where in the United States or Canada you live.

But no matter which boat you choose, let us tell you this: The only boat you need is a rowboat, with a small outboard motor if the water upon which you're going to ride is fast-moving or if your campsite is more than about a half mile from point of rental. If you'll be camping in a still-water hideaway, all you need for propulsion is the pair of oars which come with the rowboat.

The price? From about $3 to $10 a day for a rowboat without motor, about $7 to $15 a day with motor. Again, size of motor and boat and where you live are the determining factors.

You don't need a telephone book to help you rent a rowboat. Just head for the nearest fishing grounds, and in all likelihood the first place you come to that sells bait also rents rowboats from which to catch a fish. They're known by a variety of names around the country, chief among them "fishing stations," "bait stations" and "boat liveries."

## Boating Safety

Whether you intend to buy or rent, let us caution you that safe boating has its rules and regulations just as much as does safe motoring. You wouldn't, not if you're in your right mind, take a car out on the road without first learning how to drive one. Nor, doubly so, should you venture behind the controls of a boat until you know what to do and what not to do. We say doubly so because just about all of us have grown up recognizing the hazards of automobiles, but few of us know anything about the perils of boats. For example, the road cannot come up and hit you while driving a car, but the water can while driving a boat.

So by all means take a course in navigation and boating safety. In other words, qualify for your driver's license. Learn the rules of the road; learn why a power boat's operating controls are on the right and not on the left as with an automotive vehicle; learn the meaning of navigational markers; learn how tides, currents, wind and wake can affect your handling of a boat; learn all that and lots more. Then you too will be ready to venture out upon the water, the safety of your loved ones—to say nothing of your own—in your hands.

You won't, though, be ready to start right out going boat camping. First, get some expertise handling the boat, whether it's one you bought or one you rented. Safe-boating courses are conducted throughout the country by U.S. Power Boat Squadrons, chapters of the U.S. Coast Guard Auxiliary and in adult education schools. Surely one of them is available to you. Enroll and complete their course before skippering a boat. The courses usually are free.

One thing they'll teach you that bears repeating right here and now is this: Check weather reports before venturing upon the water and plan your expedition for another day if they're bad. And one thing that they may not teach you: When underway in good weather, keep a transistor radio tuned to a weather station and head for home or the nearest shore, whichever is closer, if the forecast is for a turn for the worse. Whether you buy or rent, whether you have a powerboat, a rowboat or a sailboat, you must have these things aboard every craft that ventures out upon navigable waters:

• One Coast Guard–approved life preserver (also called "flotation device") for every person aboard.

• Running lights. The regulations differ for types and sizes of craft. Make sure that your boat conforms.

- Anchor. At least one, its size depending upon the size of the craft, with line properly attached that is seven times longer than the depth of the water at high tide.
- At least one oar or paddle.
- A first-aid kit.
- Bilge pump.
- Mooring lines of various lengths.
- Signal horn, bell or whistle.
- Fire extinguisher.

Additionally, although not required by law, we think you ought also to carry these other pieces of equipment, some for safety, some for convenience, some for comfort:

- A boarding ladder for hanging over the side and climbing in and out of the boat for swimming, wading ashore or whatever. (This is a must for older, less agile people.)
- A second, smaller anchor both as a precaution and so that you can moor at right angles to the shore while camping —your regulation anchor aft, your smaller anchor set into the sand or soil by hand and with enough line so that the boat is below the low-tide line.
- Suntan lotion.
- Charts of the waters upon which you'll be cruising and camping. You'll have learned how to read them in boating class.
- Boat hook.
- Emergency food and water rations.
- A small transistor radio to keep you abreast of the weather.
- A life ring with sufficient line attached to pull a passenger back aboard if he falls overboard.
- Water bucket.
- Compass.
- Fenders.

## The Trailer Sailor

If you decide that the boat for you is one that has to be towed to the water, meaning any boat that weighs more than 150 pounds, welcome to an ever-growing fleet. The number of trailer sailors in the United States and Canada is up there somewhere in seven figures, but before you rush off to join their ranks, there are some things that you should know about boat trailers.

**The Trailer Hitch:** The same one that you have had attached to your car to pull a camping trailer also will suffice to pull a boat trailer, provided that you've followed the necessary safety rules. We cover that subject in Part II, Chapter 1, under "Wheeled Camping Vehicles." Now is the time to read it if you haven't already done so.

**The Trailer:** You'll need a trailer specifically built to pull a boat. No other will do. The trailer you buy should match the boat you've bought. Usually the same dealer can sell you both. But no matter from whom you buy your trailer, here are the points to make sure of:

• The total weight of your boat and motor should not exceed the load all commercially made trailers are rated to carry. You'll find informational plates on both boat and trailer. Match them. And find out the weight of your motor.

• The length of the trailer should be at least the length of the boat. Too short, and your transom will hang out without support and eventually cause a noticeable droop (called a "hook") in your stern that will interfere with the boat's performance and cause serious structural damage.

• Supports should be well distributed on the trailer, with the bulk of the boat's weight resting on its keel, which, in case you don't know, is the craft's main structural timber running fore and aft amidships along the very bottom.

• Transom support at the keel and chine (where the sides of the boat meet the bottom) also is a must.

• The rollers or pads supporting the bottom should be firm in their contact, but not so high that they cause a concave bubble.

• Supports should not carry too much weight; their mission is to balance the boat in transit and storage. Ideally they should meet the exterior surface at some point of interior support.

Now we come to tires. If your boat trailering is going to be limited to good road and short-distance travel to an improved launching ramp, then small-tired trailers will suffice, provided they are rated for high-speed use *and not for low-speed farm use,* in which case they will burn out and perhaps blow out after a few hundred miles.

But if you like to get off the beaten path, if you like to travel rough roads through undeveloped areas, then we urge you to consider seriously the advantages of the large wheel, preferably the same size as your car's. The advantages are these:

• Large wheels will keep the axle and body of your trailer high so you can travel rugged roads without dragging bottom.

• Large tires are also wider tires which will give you better support if launching in snow, sand or mud.

• Large tires are also high-speed tires and therefore less prone to blowouts.

• Large wheels better resist bearing burnouts.

Another possible advantage is this: If you can get a trailer whose tires and rims are the same size as those on your car, you'll not only save spare-tire storage space but also stand a better chance of purchasing a replacement if necessary in a one-garage small town.

And here is another important consideration—loaded tongue weight. The well-constructed trailer should balance your boat over its wheels, exerting only slight downward pressure on the tongue. Two factors make this a must:

• An overloaded tongue will cause both trailer and tow vehicle to swing and sway at highway speeds, thereby causing you to keep correcting your steering wheel. Not only is this annoying, tiresome and nervewracking, but also it is dangerous. Should you stop short, car and trailer could skid into a perilous jackknife.

• There will be times when you'll have to move your boat around by hand, perhaps to fit it into a tight spot for storage, or lift the tongue to load it onto your hitch.

The average-sized family car is built to take a loaded tongue weight of no more than 100 pounds, which is just about the downward pressure of a 15- or 16-foot boat. So guide yourself accordingly.

Tilt-bed trailers, though expensive, make loading and unloading a lot easier because the entire bed of the trailer tilts to meet the bottom of your boat. When the boat is winched up to a certain point, gravity takes over and the bed shifts back in line with the tongue. Lock the tilting pin in place with a pin, and you can be on your way. It's a great plus, particularly if you won't have much help in launching and loading, to say nothing of the fact that a tilt-bed trailer can be used in very shallow water.

Unless you have a boat that comes close to being a light cartopper, you'll need a trailer-mounted winch to tug the craft up onto its bed. Most commercially built trailers come with a hand winch installed. They're easy, but slow to use. If you're in a hurry or if you don't hanker for undue exertion, you can have an electric winch, provided, of course, you're willing to pay the price.

If you're packing a heavy outboard, say anything over 40 horsepower, on the back of your boat, it should not be allowed to hang down from the transom while in transit. Rather, it should be propped up.

Buy a boat trailer that has a crotched steel rod attached to it for that purpose. Simply tip the power head as far forward as it will go, tilting the lower unit into the air. Cradle that lower unit in the crotched rod and that's all there is to it.

*Make the garage your first stop after purchasing a boat trailer, and have your serviceman check your auto springs, radiator, shock absorbers, crankcase oil and the gear oil in both the transmission and the differential.*

Reason? Your car was built to pull only its own load, but reasonable additional trailer weight will do no damage if it is properly prepared for the job.

And make your service station your first stop after loading your boat onto your trailer and before you ever get started on a trip.

Reason? This time to have the attendant check both trailer and auto tires. Standard air pressures may not now be sufficient to support the load on each wheel without causing excessive sidewall flexing. Overloading the tires or running them underinflated will overheat and seriously damage them. Result? Possibly a dangerous blowout. However, with proper inflation, the tires will stay cool and safe, you'll get better gas mileage and your auto will give a more stable, comfortable ride.

**Safety and Other Points to Remember:** The chief danger points are the hitch, tires and wheel bearings. So inspect the hitch carefully every time you use it; be on the lookout for excessive looseness and for cracks or other signs of wear and tear and rusting.

• Always carry a spare, jack and lug wrench that will fit your trailer wheels.

• Use strong, adjustable tiedown straps to guard against shifting of the boat while in transit.

• Never flip a lighted cigaret out of your car window while you have a boat in tow. It could blow into your craft and fire could destroy it before you ever were aware that anything was wrong.

• When not in use, it is preferable to store the trailer (or at least the tires) indoors in order to protect the rubber from sun and weather. Tires deteriorate swiftly when constantly exposed to the elements. If you don't have a garage, use a wrap-around tarp.

• Boat launchings will cause wheel bearings to get both wet and dirty. So, particularly if hubs are driven into water, check and repack the trailer's wheel bearings several times during the boating season. In fact, it's best to check them before starting on each trip. And, even better than that, get a rig that has sealed wheel bearings.

• All trailers must be equipped with a light system hooked up to your car lights. If yours lacks the necessary plug, have your serviceman install one inside the trunk of your vehicle. And check your lights each time you start on a trip to make sure they're clearly visible and working.

• They're not mandatory, but electric brakes are good to have on your boat trailer, particularly if you'll be driving in steep country. They hook into your car's wiring just like the lights.

• Never set out on a trip without first attaching a strong safety chain to both trailer and vehicle—on the curbside of the hitch. Thus if ever the hitch fails, the trailer will be pulled away from oncoming traffic.

• Have rear-vision mirrors that will enable you to see well behind the boat trailer attached to both sides of your car.

**How to Back a Trailer:** Never venture on the road with trailer in tow until you've mastered the fine art of backing up. Best time and place to practice is in a shopping-center parking lot on a Sunday afternoon. When backing, always take it slow, while doing this:

• Turn your steering wheel to the right to start the trailer turning left, or vice versa.

• Then gradually straighten out as the trailer heads in the direction you want it to go.

• Backing over a long distance will require frequent corrections. When correcting, again be sure to turn your wheel in the opposite direction from which you want the trailer to go.

• Don't ever let the trailer angle more than 45 degrees from your rear bumper. If it goes beyond that point, pull forward to straighten out and start over again. Otherwise you'll jackknife.

• Pay no attention to your car wheels. Watch only what your trailer is doing.

If all of that sounds too tiresome, too tedious, here's a simple solution: Mount a hitch on your front as well as on your rear bumper. Then instead of backing up, unhitch the trailer from the rear bumper, turn your car around and attach the trailer to your front bumper. Then drive forward and the trailer goes backward exactly where you want it to go.

*Before guiding your boat trailer down a launching ramp, attach a long length of line—at least 30 feet—to the nose of the craft. And make sure that you or someone else hangs on to the rope as the boat slides off into the water, while standing well above the ramp's wet, slippery surface. That way,*

*not only will you always have the boat under control once it's in the water, but the person holding the line won't suddenly find his feet sliding out from under him as the boat drifts out with the tide, current or wind.*

**Camping Equipment and How to Stow It:** The first part of this heading can be summed up in this one sentence: The camping equipment you'll need or want on a weekend boat camping trip is exactly the same as the equipment you'd need or want on any weekend camping trip. If space and weight are problems, backpacking equipment will help you solve it. So we refer to Chapters 2 through 6 of Part II of this book. Chapter 4 of Part II talks about food to take along, and here now we'll add only this one note: Take a bit less if you're sure that where you are going you will also catch fish. You'll find fish cooked over a campfire the moment it's caught is the finest-tasting food you've ever eaten, no matter what the meal, breakfast, dinner or supper. You say you don't like fish? Read the many different ways to prepare fish in our two fish cookbooks—*The Savor of the Sea* and *The Complete Fish Cookbook.* And follow our fish cooking directions in the recipe section of this book and you'll be in for the gastronomical find of your life.

So now here's how to stow your camping gear while aboard a boat.

• Pack everything, including food and cooking and eating utensils, that you don't want to get wet from spray or accidental dunking, in either canvas duffel bags or heavy plastic sacks. This will also make such unwieldy things as stoves and chemical toilets easier to handle.

• Do not step from shore or dock into the boat with anything in your hands. Instead, stand in the boat and reach across for bags one by one or have someone hand them to you.

• In larger boats stow them under the bow deck, seats and whatever other storage compartments may be built into the craft. Anything too large for such places—your bagged tent, for instance—should be laid in the cockpit as much forward of amidships and as out of the way as possible.

• In smaller boats that have no such storage areas, you have no choice but to stow everything forward of amidships.

If your gear and passengers overcrowd the craft, make two trips. Three, if necessary. We can't overemphasize how hazardous it can be, no matter how calm the weather and the water, for boats to be overloaded.

*This is as good a place as any to tell you this: Every boat has, or should have, a manufacturer's capacity-load plate attached somewhere within easy view. These plates tell you both the maximum weight and the number of passengers the craft should carry. But, if you'd rather be safe than sorry, you'll stay at least one-quarter below those maximum-capacity figures. Especially in number of passengers.*

**How to Unload Cargo and Moor at Campsite:** Run the nose of your boat as far up on the beach as possible while still leaving the propeller of your downtilted motor in the water.

• If the boat is large enough to necessitate use of a ladder, hang one over the side.

• All but one person (that one being able to operate the boat) climb ashore, one of them taking a small anchor that you've already attached to a bow cleat and setting it by hand into the beach sand or soil. If you have no such second anchor, tie a mooring line to a tree, log, stump or whatever.

• Now hand your gear over the side, piece by piece, to your shorebound stevedores.

• If you are in still, nontidal water, uptilt your motor, set your stern anchor so that the boat will remain bow into the beach no matter what the turn of the wind or the weather, and climb ashore.

• If in running tidal water, have someone pay out the bow-anchor line while you back off the beach until you are surely below the low-tide line. Now set your stern anchor and have your bow hand take up the slack in the anchor line.

• All that's now left for you to do is go over the side and either wade or swim ashore (or pull yourself in hand-over-hand on the bow-anchor line) and help set up camp.

**Where to Make Camp:** Maybe we told you this before, but we'll tell you again: Set up camp on a high spot—well above the mosquito and bug line, well above the high-water line, well above and out of the path of runoff water in case it rains. Also, if possible, well above the morning-mist line.

**A Word About Shelter:** If you are camping in a really isolated spot, far removed from passersby and prying eyes, and if you're sure that the weather will remain nice for the duration of your stay, you don't really need a tent for nighttime shelter. There's no nicer way of sleeping under the stars than with nothing between you and them but the clear, clear night. Just snuggle yourself in your sleeping bag, or other bed gear (perhaps covered with a mosquito net), and enjoy a peek at the heavens between the leafy branches of the trees.

Or, if you feel that you need some sort of shelter and your boat is light enough to so handle, just tip it up on one gunwale at a 45-degree angle, prop it firmly in place with a couple of paddles or sturdy lengths of wood, and that's all the shelter you need.

Or, if you want still more than that, just drape a light tarpaulin or blanket at an opposite 45-degree angle and you have a pup tent. (See page 75 for more details.) It's a quick way of getting out of a sudden rainstorm, too. So don't knock it.

# Chapter 2

## Canoe Camping

If you'd like a taste of how the lake and river Indians once moved from place to place, camping as they went, then you'll by all means have to have a canoe.

A canoe will go just about anywhere that any other boat will go, but—and this is the one thing that makes it something special—a canoe also will go places that no other vehicle would dare. Not by land, not by water. In the back country, the wild country. Places that have never known the sight of a sail, the stench of a motor. These are the primitive areas, some of which still remain in these tarnished-by-man 50 United States.

Canoeing also is a grand form of exercise, not quite so strenuous as rowing but decidedly more muscle-building than sailing and motorboating. So, until you get your muscles in tune, until you develop the skill and the stamina, if you are to answer the call of the wild, we'd suggest that you confine your canoeing and your canoe camping to slow-running streams, placid ponds, quiet lakes.

### The Canoe for You

No longer, unless you have it custom-made and we're not even sure of that, can you buy a bark canoe of the kind the Indians fashioned with great skill when forests stood tall and trees were plentiful throughout the land. Today, however, with canoeing increasing in popularity, you can buy or rent canoes made of fiberglass, wood and canvas or aluminum. Our preference is for the latter and we'll tell you why.

Grumman, the same company that makes moon-exploration vehicles and Navy airplanes, is a pioneer in the aluminum-canoe field, turning out its first one more than a quarter century ago and applying to canoes the same engineering know-how that it does to lunar probes. Today Grumman canoes are better than ever because the company has developed a marine aluminum that stands up wonderfully well under saltwater and salt-air conditions with a minimum of care; they contain flotation that makes them unsinkable; the smallest aluminum canoe, a 13-footer, weighs only 44 pounds, the largest, a 20-footer, only 117 pounds, and so they are easily cartopped or portaged; the smallest of them cost less than $250, the largest less than $400; they're easy to maintain; all of them can be turned into sailboats with not much more than a twist of a screwdriver; all of them are made so that small outboard motors can easily be attached.

Canoes range in length, depending upon the manufacturer, from about 12 feet to about 22 feet. Some are double-ended, others have square sterns and can be either rowed or paddled. All, as with all other boats, should carry capacity plates that will let you know their safe-load limits. For example, the Grumman 13-footer has a recommended load limit of 590 pounds whether the poundage is made up of people, camping gear, three-horsepower motor or a combination of all of them. Therefore, says Grumman, it can safely carry three people and that is where we differ: We recommend for certainty's sake that you reduce capacity-plate load limits by one-quarter, which brings our ceiling down to about 450 pounds or two people plus camping gear.

*The reason for our urging you always to cut down from the manufacturer's load limits has to do with an emergency life-and-death decision that every boatman may someday have to make in a split second. With that in mind let us ask you this: The capacity plate says that the craft can safely carry, let's say, three people, and so you put out from shore with your young son and your young daughter aboard; then suddenly a giant cruiser tears by, a crazy at the helm, and its wake swamps your boat, throwing both youngsters into the water. You can only reach to save one, your son or your daughter. Which will it be?*

*We don't ask you to answer that question. Rather, we ask you always to bear such a question in mind every time you step into a boat, whether it be a canoe, a rowboat, a sailboat or a motorboat.*

*So now is a good place to add this stipulation to our warning never to load beyond three-quarters of capacity: Make your weight reduction not in gear, but in people. In other words, if the load-capacity plate says four people, carry only three including yourself; if it says five, carry only four; if it says six, carry five. If it says more than six, split your party into two canoes.*

Many boat dealers also sell canoes. Additionally, you'll find canoe dealers in the yellow pages. If you prefer to rent rather than buy, the phone book will tell you where that can be done, too. Or you can write to Grumman Boats, Marathon, N.Y. 13803, and ask for a free copy of its Rent-a-Canoe Directory which covers all of the United States and Canada, broken down by states and provinces. Many boat liveries also rent camping gear, so it is possible to kill two birds with one stone.

## Paddles

Paddles are made of both aluminum and various types of wood, including pine, hickory, ash and spruce. Our preference is for a good grade of airplane spruce, because it is light, has a little give and feels good to the touch. When choosing yours, select paddles with straight grains and examine them carefully for signs of splitting. It's best, too, that the blades be capped with lead or copper tips to keep them from cracking from repeated contact with gravel, rocks, dirt and other earthly—and man-made—substances, including beer cans and soda bottles.

Canoe paddles should be of different lengths, one for the

bowman, and the other for the sternman who will be doing the steering and therefore will require a longer paddle. A good rule of thumb, or rather torso, is to pick a bow paddle that reaches from the ground to your shoulder and a stern paddle that reaches from the ground to your eyes.

## Outboard Motors for Canoes

Motors and canoes are not by nature meant for each other, but still it's a good idea to have one along for a variety of reasons, chief among them when the water is running downriver and your destination is upriver. Then there are extraneous other reasons, among them that you may want to do some trolling for fish. Then a motor is ideal.

Most double-ended canoes made today can have a motor mount clamped onto one side near the aft end, so power-propelling one of them is no problem. As for square-stern canoes, the only reason that we know of for that blunt aft end is to accommodate a motor.

What size motor? We'd say three horsepower for a boat up to 13 feet, five horsepower up to 18 feet, seven and a half horsepower up to 20 feet and no more than ten horsepower for any canoe that's longer than that.

## Canoe Equipment You Must Have or Should Have

As with any other kind of boating, whether you own or rent a canoe, if you want your voyage to be safe, you must or should have this equipment:

• One Coast Guard–approved life jacket for each occupant.

• Coast Guard–approved buoyant cushions that can double as life preservers for sitting on.

• A three-pound anchor and sufficient line to cope with any contingency.

• Signal horn, bell or whistle.

• An extra paddle.

- Compass.
- A waterproof pull-cord bag that you can tie to a thwart and in which you can stow your wallet, watch and similar valuables.
- A strong long-beam light.
- A waterproof plastic tarpaulin with grommets under which you can stow your gear and to use as a shelter.
- Foam pontoons that clamp onto the gunwales amidships to provide extra stability. They're particularly helpful when used with a side-bracket outboard motor.
- Floorboards.
- Carrying yokes that clamp to gunwales over center thwart to make portaging more comfortable.
- Backrests for passengers.
- Cartop carrier rack and tie-downs if that's the way you're going to get your canoe from home to water.
- Bow and stern lines, each at least the length of the canoe, for mooring and towing if ever you hit a stretch of unnavigable water (as you probably will), so that you can walk along the shore pulling the canoe along beside you.

An excellent variation of the tow lines, by the way, is one length of line long enough to tie to both ends of the canoe and still allow enough of a yoke for one man to maneuver from shore.

## Canoe Camping Gear

As we said earlier on in this book, the idea in camping is always to travel light. The less you have in the way of gear, the easier your outing will be and the happier you will be.

Most canoes will not accommodate so much cargo as will most cars, but still the load limits that we spoke of will permit you to carry as much as needed. However, how much you'll need and what you will need is strictly up to you. One person's necessities are another person's luxuries. So it is for you to decide what you should lug along from the camping-gear lists that we gave in Part II, Chapter 6.

But before you do decide, our advice to you is that you'd better know where you're going to camp on canoe journey's

end and what kind of obstacles you are going to encounter
in between start and stop. For example, are you going to encounter white water? Are you going to shoot any rapids? Are
you going to have to portage (which means, in case you don't
know, to carry) all your gear, including canoe, from one
navigable stretch of water to another?

If your trip is definitely not going to encounter any such
obstacles, then feel free to take along even a thermos jug
full of cocktails. But if you're going to have to portage a
mile or two, then perhaps you won't want much more than
you can carry on your back. Only you will know the answers.

**How to Stow Your Gear:** The trick in canoeing is to present as low a silhouette as possible to the wind. The lower
the load, including both people and cargo, the less of a
surface you'll present for the wind to grab hold of and kick
around like a kite.

So here's the first rule in stowing your camping gear: Keep
everything below the gunwales.

Here's the second rule: Stow everything behind the
canoe's center thwart, thus shifting the center of gravity
to one or two feet behind the craft's midship point. This will
raise the bow and dig in the stern, thus allowing for greater
control and maneuverability when under way.

And here's the third rule: Lash all of your cargo to the
canoe to prevent both the weight from shifting and the loss
of gear should the craft tip. Best way to do this is first to
wrap everything in the waterproof plastic tarp that we told
you to take along. Besides keeping your things dry and neatly
tucked in, the tarp can be used later in camp either as a dining fly or as a shelter, the latter being best accomplished like
this: Just prop your canoe up on one gunwale, angle the tarp
down from it in the other direction, secure it with stakes, and
you have all the tent you'll need for a one- or two-night camping trip. Not luxurious, but adequate.

## Canoeing Safety

Safety in a canoe begins before you ever board one. First,
although there is no law that says you must, you ought to

wear a pair of lightweight nonskid shoes, preferably a pair of boat sneakers. Second, if you can't swim for at least ten minutes while fully clothed, you'd better wear a life jacket. So, too, for everyone who is going canoeing with you, especially children. They should wear life jackets whether they can swim or not.

Now, properly shod, properly jacketed, the next thing is to be able to get into a canoe without its slipping out from under you. Here's how, if the craft is alongside a dock or pier:

- Bend low or kneel while facing the bow.
- Grasp the near gunwale with the hand that's nearest it.
- Place the foot nearest the canoe on the bottom of the craft directly over its centerline.
- Shift hands so that you are now grasping both gunwales.
- Bring the other foot aboard.
- Move to your paddling position by keeping your body crouched low and sliding your hands along the gunwale.

Here's how to board a canoe from shore:

- Swing the craft so its stern rests on the shore, its end barely touching the bottom.
- The stern paddler stands on shore facing the water, straddles the canoe with his legs and braces it against rocking with his knees and hands.
- The bow paddler steps around him, places his near foot carefully into the center of the canoe as far forward as safely possible, grasps a gunwale in each hand, swings the other foot aboard and, crouching low (his hands still holding the gunwale), crab-crawls along the centerline until reaching his paddling position on the far end of the canoe.
- Now, with the bowman holding the canoe steady with his paddle, the sternman shoves the craft gently a foot or so from shore, grasps both gunwales and steps aboard one foot at a time.

Passengers, if any, board the canoe in the same way. And once underway, no one should stand up or move from one position in the craft to another. If it is necessary to move, then do so by sliding along the bottom on your buttocks or by grasping the gunwales and crouching low almost in a crawling position.

No one, not passengers, not paddlers, should sit in the thwarts or on the seats that some canoes (for reasons unknown to us) have built into them. Always sit on the bottom. The best position for paddling is kneeling, either on both knees or on one; if the latter, with your other leg extended forward. Not only does kneeling keep paddlers low, it also gives them a more powerful stroke.

Some other safety rules to remember and abide by:

• If the weather or water suddenly turns bad, everyone should don life jackets.

• At the first sign of a sudden squall, make for the nearest shore, beach your canoe and stay on dry ground above and away from the water until the storm passes. If it's an electrical storm, stay away from tall trees, or other high or metal objects, and lie down so that *you* won't be a high object that might attract the lightning.

• If a squall hits before there is time to paddle to shore, lie down in the canoe and thus keep low until it blows over.

• If the canoe fills with water ("swamp" is the word for it) for some reason, stay in it. It won't sink. But bail the water out, of course, either by rocking from side to side or by using a bucket, can, hat or whatever.

• If the canoe turns over ("capsize" is the word for it), don't attempt to swim to shore. A capsized canoe will float, so cling to it until help arrives.

• When underway, it's best to paddle as close as possible to the lee shore, where you are most protected from the wind.

• If a person falls overboard, he can climb back into the canoe by reaching across the gunwale amidships, keeping his head low and pressing the palms of his hands down on the bottom of the canoe, kicking his feet to the surface of the water, continuing to press with the hands and kick with the feet until the canoe is under the torso, and the head, still kept low, touches the opposite side, and finally rolling over into a sitting position in the bottom of the canoe.

• The most important safety rule we can give you is to become expert in all aspects of canoe handling before you even think of a canoe camping trip.